Second Start

Second Start

Bobby Beasley

W. H. Allen · London

A Howard & Wyndham Company
1976

© BOBBY BEASLEY AND TIM FITZGEORGE-PARKER, 1976

THIS BOOK OR PARTS THEREOF MAY NOT BE REPRODUCED
WITHOUT PERMISSION IN WRITING.
PRINTED AND BOUND IN GREAT BRITAIN BY
THE GARDEN CITY PRESS LIMITED, LETCHWORTH, HERTFORDSHIRE
SG6 1JS, FOR THE PUBLISHERS, W. H. ALLEN & CO. LTD,
44 HILL STREET, LONDON W1X 8LB

ISBN 0 491 01985 8

for my children
Caroline, Peter and Helen

Acknowledgements

When I decided to tell my story, I sought help from my old friend, the distinguished horseman/writer, Tim Fitzgeorge-Parker. As a former steeplechase rider and trainer, he knows every aspect of the racing world and, from a profound study of human nature, he understands all the problems that I have encountered. I am delighted with this book and would like to express my gratitude to Tim for all his hard work and sympathy.

I would like to thank the following newspapers for their permission to quote extracts: *The Observer*, *The Daily Telegraph*, the *Sunday Telegraph*, the *Daily Express*, the *Sunday Express* and the *Daily Mirror*.

I also wish to extend my sincere thanks to Fred Winter for the wonderful foreword, which I certainly don't deserve.
Bobby Beasley

Contents

Dear Bobby

Thank you for asking me to write the Foreword to your book.

Ironically two great racing triumphs of your comeback, the Sweeps Hurdle and the Gold Cup, were gained at the expense of my horses, Bula and Pendil, both of which should have been ridden by you as my stable jockey. But no one applauded them more than I, who knew that you had finally won the battle over alcoholism, the terrible disease which caused you to leave me and to quit the profession at which you excelled.

Although I am naturally flattered and gratified by your praise and by your comments on my kindness and tolerance in saying that your job as first jockey would always be there waiting for you, believe me my motives were not so unselfish. I had offered you the job in the first place for one very good reason. I knew, from personal experience of riding against you over the years, that you were one of the best. Your style, strength, horseman-ship, intelligence, dedication and above all, your intense will to win made you as hard as any man to beat.

It took me some months to recognise the nature of your problem. I could not understand the fluctuations in your riding. One day you would be the old Bobby at his brilliant best. The next would find you uninspired, feeble or downright bad by your standards.

When I realised the cause of the tragedy that had befallen you and your family, I thought, as everyone should, that there, but for the grace of God, go I, because I knew that you were genuinely ill, that alcoholism is a disease and not weakness of character. So I wanted you, sober and rehabilitated, to return and ride my best horses. Your form in your comeback filled me with admiration and proved me right.

Your story will not only give new heart to alcoholics all over the world and help others to an understanding of the disease, but it will also expose to young jockeys and, indeed, to all young people the pitfalls and stark tragedy into which drink can lead them.

You have such a great understanding of horses that, if you return to racing as a trainer, I will fear your horses as much as I feared those ridden by you as my rival. But in the meantime I am delighted to hear that you are building up your dairy herd and wish you all the success that you so richly deserve.

With kindest regards to Shirley and your family,

Yours sincerely

Fred Winter

Just for Today

JUST FOR TODAY I will try to live through this day only, and not tackle all my problems at once. I can do something for twelve hours that would appal me if I felt that I had to keep it up for a lifetime.

JUST FOR TODAY I will be happy. This assumes to be true what Abraham Lincoln said, that 'Most folks are as happy as they make up their minds to be'.

JUST FOR TODAY I will adjust myself to what is, and not try to adjust everything to my own desires. I will take my 'luck' as it comes, and fit myself to it.

JUST FOR TODAY I will try to strengthen my mind, I will study, I will learn something useful. I will not be a mental loafer, I will read something that requires effort, thought and concentration.

JUST FOR TODAY I will exercise my soul in three ways: I will do somebody a good turn, and not get found out: if anybody knows of it, it will not count. I will do at least two things I

13

don't want to do—just for exercise. I will not show anyone that my feelings are hurt: they may be hurt, but today I will not show it.

JUST FOR TODAY I will be agreeable. I will look as well as I can, dress becomingly, keep my voice low, be courteous, criticise not one bit. I won't find fault with anything, nor try to improve or regulate anybody but myself.

JUST FOR TODAY I will have a programme. I may not follow it exactly, but I will have it. I will save myself from two pests: hurry and indecision.

JUST FOR TODAY I will have a quiet half hour all by myself, and relax. During this half hour, sometime, I will try to get a better perspective of my life.

JUST FOR TODAY I will be unafraid. Especially I will not be afraid to enjoy what is beautiful, and to believe that as I give to the world, so the world will give to me.

Prayer for Today

Lord, make me an instrument of Thy peace. Where there is hatred, let me sow love: where there is injury, pardon: where there is doubt, faith: where there is despair, hope: where there is darkness, light, and where there is sadness, joy.

O, Divine Master, grant that I may not so much seek to be consoled, as to console: to be understood, as to understand: to be loved, as to love: for it is in giving that we receive, it is in pardoning that we are pardoned, and it is in dying that we are born to eternal life.

I'd done it; made the comeback, won the big one, the Irish Sweeps Hurdle. I pulled up and turned Christy round to walk back through the cheering crowds; as I had done so often before. But this time I barely saw them. 'My name is Bobby. I am an alcoholic. . . .' No elation. I must feel no elation. This leads to celebration and celebration means temptation to drink. More cheers, smile, but mind blank.

'Well done, Bobby! That's the stuff!' shouts an Irish trainer, who had been one of my worst detractors and had never lifted a finger to help me when I was down. The two-faced bastard! Forget it. No resentment. Anger only leads to drink.

'My name is Bobby. I am an alcoholic. . . .' Mechanically I ride towards the unsaddling enclosure and scarcely see the happy lad, who seizes the bridle and fastens the lead rein. I hardly recognise Pat Taaffe grinning all over the cheery, rosy face I knew so well, or the owner and his wife. I've just done my job as well as I could.

'Well done, Mate!' I turn and see the scarlet and pale blue colours of Bula, the favourite, as Paul Kelleway trots up to join me. I'd beaten him so easily.

CHAPTER I

Comeback

The Press called it, 'the Biggest Comeback since Lazarus'. I won't argue. After all it was barely eighteen months since I'd ridden my first winner after my enforced retirement. I was back again riding as a full-time jockey and my old friend Pat Taaffe, who will always be associated with Arkle, had retained me to ride Captain Christy in all his races. We had already had a fair bit of success and Pat, as ambitious as ever, was talking about the Irish Sweeps Hurdle and the Champion Hurdle at Cheltenham a long time before Christmas.

The Irish Sweeps Hurdle, like the Irish Sweeps Derby, is an imaginative race which has fully justified all the enthusiasm of its sponsors. It has the biggest stake of any hurdle race in Ireland or England. English owners and trainers of jumpers, having to exist on rotten prize money, were naturally attracted. This year the Sweeps Hurdle had attracted the best. When I went to Leopardstown on Boxing Day in 1972 I knew that against all the odds I must have a bit of a squeak.

I was thirty-seven years old, which is normally past the best age for a jumping jockey, but I somehow felt that I had started on a new career. The past had definitely been worth while. It

17

was a most impressive line-up, including no less than the top European hurdlers, Bula and Comedy of Errors. No Irish horse had won the race before and there was tremendous excitement heightened by the normal Christmas celebrations in Ireland. Everyone was talking about it.

It is extraordinary how in Ireland the mind seems to go towards racing, whatever other subject is being spoken about. Of course bloodstock is the major industry, unlike England, where they have steel and motor cars. There was that day when the first journey into space took place. While the Russian Sputnik was circling around in space, some Irish friends were drinking in a Dublin hotel. At this time there were several jockeys who were well known for their technique at giving a horse 'an easy race'. The conversation had had nothing to do with racing but was entirely concerned with this extraordinary little machine circling the world.

'How on earth do you think they'll ever stop it?' asked someone. With no hesitation at all someone else said, 'Won't they send——up there?' naming a celebrated jockey!

So here we were at Christmas with this great race coming up. The Press was full of it. Not only was England sending over the dual Champion Hurdler and his challenger, but all the best candidates in Ireland were engaged. There was so much excitement.

Before we went off to Leopardstown I had a long talk with Pat about tactics. Great jockey that he had been, he had never ridden regularly in England as I had. I knew Paul Kelleway from old and I had watched him ride Bula in England. I knew from earlier days that he was always inclined to be a bit cocky and a bit arrogant in his riding, although not in his normal life. I remember one day at Warwick when we were crowding together over the second hurdle, I felt a hand come up between my thighs and the saddle and catch hold of my balls. 'How are you going, matey?' said a voice from behind. There was Paul, grinning all over his face. Fortunately he let go before we had to jump the hurdle. And I knew that for some reason best known to himself, he liked to lie out of his ground and come with a late flourish to win in the most dramatic way. This was partly because he liked to tease his trainer, Fred Winter, and partly because he loved the thrill of it all.

Now, knowing Paul as well as I did, I reckoned it was the first time he had come to Leopardstown, and that he possibly thought that the racing over in Ireland was pretty cushy and that the jockeys were tulips. So Pat and I had a chat and worked out a strategy. In his two races, Captain Christy had made the running and had gone at a hell of a gallop. He was a good jumper and stayer and, once he got going, it appeared that he couldn't be caught.

So I reckoned that Paul was almost certain to lie out of his ground, prepared to come with a late flourish and make all of us Irish yokels look idiots. I told Pat, 'There's only one chance we have here. And that's to jump off and go like hell. When we get over on the far side in the back straight with about a mile to go, I'll try and slip the field. Knowing that Paul will probably want to come with a late run and get through on the inside, I'm fairly happy. I have a lot of experience of the track and I know that he won't be able to get through on that long turn into the straight even if the ones in front are dying.' Pat agreed, and I cantered down to the start at Leopardstown with a confidence that I hadn't felt for years.

I heard Paul Kelleway say to the starter, 'Oh! don't take any notice of me. I'm in no hurry to jump off. I'll drop in behind them.'

I thought to myself that the plan was going to work. I jumped Captain Christy out of the gate and set off at a hell of a good gallop. I looked round and couldn't see any sign of Bula anywhere. I congratulated myself. This is great, I thought. With a mile to go I gave Christy a kick, and he opened up a lead of many lengths. As we turned into the straight we were unassailable, and he stayed on strongly to beat Comedy of Errors by a very long-looking six lengths. I kept him going well until he passed the post and then, as I had always been taught, trotted him right out. So many good horses have started breakdowns by being pulled up too sharply after the finish. As I rode back, I thought that I had done a good job and that I had earned my first bit of real money for some time. Money which would help me to build a new cow-house down on the farm in Co. Wexford. But I felt no elation. This was the first few quid I had got since my return. I said to myself that I must try not to make the same mistakes I had made before. When a red-faced trainer patted my horse and shouted: 'Well done, Bobby!', there was the temptation to remember that only a short while ago he had been one of my worst detractors. But instead of saying: 'You stupid bastard!' I just smiled. I had learnt that resentment brings anger, and anger brings drink.

I dismounted, acknowledged all the cheers of the crowd—which were fantastic—and weighed in. 'Winner all right!' they announced. I wasn't interested in the congratulations. I just wanted to get off home to Wexford. There was no party, no booze, no celebration, because I had learnt from Alcoholics Anonymous that you must try to have no highs and no lows. Having seen it all before, I realised that the good days were the danger and not the bad days. I had been through the mill, raced for a long time, ridden many winners, and been Champion Jockey. The celebrations had been long and drunken. The high life very high. But not any more. Now I must not make the same mistakes: I realised that I had been given a second chance and I was going to try to cash in on it. My racing life wasn't going to last much longer because I was already thirty-seven years old. So I must make as much as I could, seek stability, and build something for the future. I had my farm, which I had bought from winning the Grand National on Nicolaus Silver eleven years earlier. Now I was determined that everything I got from racing would be used to build it up.

I got into my car and drove home. Irish drivers are terrible, but the roads were fairly deserted at this time. People were either at the races, hunting, or sleeping off the effect of Christmas in front of television. It's a sad reflection on my home country that in most of those funny little towns every other building seems to be a chemist, a betting shop or a pub. As I drove through one of those towns, I saw a pub I had known very well from the old days. Two years earlier I would have stopped there for sure. Now I wasn't tempted at all. I thought yet again of the tragedy of Ireland's vast increase in alcoholism.

As I drove, I relived the race. I was already looking at it objectively, planning for the future. Captain Christy was clearly better than Pat and I had thought. We must be real champions. I believed that even if we had not out-manoeuvred Paul Kelleway, we would still have beaten Bula, winner of two Champion Hurdles. Bula, the burly brown horse with the bold head, was the last animal I had ridden when I reached rock-bottom in those last days at Lambourn. I had given up the finest job in my racing world, as first jockey to Fred Winter, and had, as I thought, hung up my racing boots for good.

I had been hanging around Lambourn for a bit and Fred had said: 'You may as well ride out to pass the time and keep you amused. It'll keep you off the booze a bit.' So I used to go down there and, although I didn't give a damn about anything, I rode out on this young horse, whom the lads called 'the cob'—a sort of hunter-type animal. He was kept in the bottom yard, and he was fat with no shape about him at that time. Certainly he didn't look anything. We used a field in Upper Lambourn opposite Peter Nelson's yard, where the 1974 Derby Winner, Snow Knight, was trained. After the corn was cut there was quite a lot of stubble, and provided one watched out for cracked heels, we could exercise all the young horses there in a group of, say ten, at a time. They were just learning what it was all about, how to go straight and whether they had any speed or not.

The field sloped upwards towards the Mann Down gallops, giving a nice gentle hill. So we used to speed these unmade young horses up the hill. This 'cob', Bula, always used to finish about ten lengths in front of them. It was so easy, and his speed was so remarkable, that the lads couldn't believe it. They used to laugh and say it was just a fluke. However, two Champion Hurdles proved it was no fluke. But now I had beaten him, and the sight of this great little horse took me right back to the beginning.

CHAPTER 2

The White Blackbird

It was a white blackbird which started the trouble for the Beasleys. My great-grandfather was a Protestant and my grandmother was constantly trying to persuade him to turn Roman Catholic. Eventually, nagged beyond reason by his wife and daughter, the old man made an impish concession.

'All right,' he said on a Sunday, when the women had returned from Mass, feeling particularly holy and had pressurised him again. 'I promise to become a Catholic the day I shoot a white blackbird.'

They had to be content with that and no doubt he thought he was safe. He kept a shot-gun in his bedroom, and one morning had the satisfaction of shooting a dove through the bathroom window. Perhaps he felt he was striking a blow at the R.C. Church, with its doves and incense, but then my grandmother went out to pick up the dead bird, and brought it back in triumph. It was an albino blackbird. We still have it stuffed at home, and many's the time I've called it names and cursed it for changing our way of life. That bird set up a chain reaction which was to have a profound influence on my character.

Despite all the troubles, the pattern of life in Ireland has, until very recently, remained fairly uniform as far as the country's chief industries, racing and breeding, are concerned. The top men, the rich owners and breeders, the Turf Club members, were mainly Protestants. For long there has been the extraordinary anomaly whereby those bred and equipped by ability, money and position to lead, have taken no part in the government of the Country where they live and employ so much labour. They enjoy a happy, carefree social sporting life, paying minimal taxes as long as they continue to promote the Irish horse throughout the world. Now at last politicians like Cosgrove and Haughey have started to bridge the gap, and other Catholics of the calibre of Vincent O'Brien have gained immense power and influence in the land. The funny thing was that we regarded these Protestant landed gentry as being Irish, although, of course, they were mostly Anglo-Irish at best. They were all educated in England and enjoyed the best of both worlds.

Sir Gordon Richards was talking recently about my father. 'Harry Beasley,' he said, 'was brilliant. No one who didn't ride against him will ever realise quite what an outstanding jockey he was. I did and I know. None better. He wasn't just a jockey but a strong, beautiful horseman.' My Uncle Pat, better known in England as Rufus, had a long, successful career as a jockey. He was for many years associated with Sir Cecil Boyd-Rochfort's stable. He won the St Leger on Boswell, and the Ascot Gold Cup on Precipitation. From 1946 until 1974 he trained at Malton in Yorkshire, winning the Cambridgeshire three times, the Royal Hunt Cup, the Wokingham, the Middle Park, the Zetland Gold Cup, the Manchester November Handicap and many other races. He was, and is, justifiably, a very popular man. I have always liked the story of Uncle Pat at one of those big posh parties in Yorkshire. They had been discussing some lady whom one of the guests apparently admired. In one of those silences that so often occur, Rufus was heard to remark, in his soft, carrying Irish voice, 'Imagine!

24

You find that one attractive? I wouldn't fuck her for practice!'
His host and neighbour, Major John Shaw, immediately named
two of his fillies, 'Imagine' and 'Practice'. They became founda-
tion mares for his successful little stud at Kirby Moorside.

Yes, I suppose Beasley is one of the most famous names in
racing. My grandfather and my uncle both won the National.
Back in the 1890s they won four Nationals between them. My
grandfather won over fences, hurdles and on the flat. He rode
his last winner when he was eighty-three. Dad came to England
soon after the end of the First World War, and for several
seasons rode for his old friend Atty Persse, winning the Two
Thousand Guineas for the stable in 1929 on Mr Jinks.

For a short while after his retirement as a jockey, we were
among the rich in an impoverished country. But, always, hanging over Ireland was the shadow of the Roman Catholic
Church. Only in Spain has it as much influence, and many find
it hard to explain. Perhaps Bruce Marshall summed it up best
when, in one of his later books, *Thread of Scarlet*, he
described a young Scottish priest, summoned to attend the
dying throes of drunken Irishmen in the gutters of Glasgow.
Unable to give a man the last rites according to the Book, the
priest would say, 'Well, as you can't say anything else, say
"Jesus, mercy!"' The poor fellow would raise his head for
one last moment, say 'Jesus, Murphy!' and die 'safe in the
embrace of the Emerald Church'. It is so different from the
R.C. Church in England, France or the United States, that
only those of us who have lived there as Catholics know what
an influence that 'Emerald Church' wielded. It's almost un-
believable. My first recollection of the strict religious upbringing that was to have such an effect on me as an adolescent was
when I was sent to Killashee Convent school outside Naas, at
the age of five. It was very strict and puritanical. One of the
rules, which I remember well—and which possibly had some
psychological effect on me later on—was that we had to wear
bathing suits every time we had a bath. We were told that
angels might get shocked at seeing us in the nude. To show

you how insecure I felt at this time, I actually ran away from this small convent at the age of five. I can still remember being taken there, and my parents arguing over something, so violently, I suppose, that even at that age I felt I had to get back to see whether they were still together. They were, but the incident seemed to influence my stability later in life. At that early age you need love, care and protection. Killashee was the 'in' convent of the time, and it's still going. I must admit I hated it.

My brother went there, and one particular incident had a profound effect on him in later life. Until he was six years old he still occasionally wet his bed. When he did this he was made to wash his sheets in public because it was, apparently, a terrible thing to do.

I suppose that from an early age I developed a feeling against the clerical type of teaching which I was destined to go through. I attended a number of convents and was constantly being brain-washed with a way of life in which one did what one was told. I was brought up with a narrow, puritanical outlook. We were segregated from the girls. We never mixed. There was always the feeling of 'them' and 'us'. Even up to a very few years ago in Ireland, if you went to church, you had women on one side and men on the other. You went to a dance, and the men were on one side and the women on the other.

My brother went to confession in church at the age of fourteen. 'Bless me, Father, for I have sinned and it is two weeks since my last confession. During this time I have masturbated.' Through the grille thundered the voice of the priest. 'Get out of this church. You are damned for ever. Never come back again!'

I was eleven when, one Sunday, in a convent, we were all dolled up in our best for Mass, with the girls on one side and the boys on the other as usual. The girls looked smart in their nice red tunics and blouses, and even at that age I had the stirrings of normal male interest in females. But there was always a nun on duty, patrolling up and down the aisle saying: 'No eyes for the girls or you're in trouble.'

We moved about a lot and never had much sense of belonging to a place. I went to a number of different Roman Catholic schools. There, and at home, the priests were omnipotent. We R.C's were forbidden to eat meat on Friday and poor parishioners ate small bits of cod, or just potatoes. But you would find the black-suited, dog-collared priests, sticking to the rules of course, tucking in to salmon, lobster and Dublin Bay prawns in expensive restaurants.

Because they exerted so much influence in the schools, I reckon they must take a lot of the blame for the present troubles in Ireland. Although my father and mother were thoroughly Anglicised, I was brought up at school to detest the English. By the time I went to England for the first time, at the age of eight, during the war this had been refined to a tremendous hatred. As Uncle Rufus would say, 'Imagine! Doing that to a boy of that age!' It was pretty evil when you think about it, and with me it almost took on a practical form. My parents found me sharpening a little knife I had bought. 'What are you doing with that knife, Bobby?' they asked. And I answered, 'I'm going to gut every Englishman I see because I hate them.' All this I learnt, along with the Irish language, in school. Hatred of the English was the only acceptable thing, and in the forties and fifties Irish schools were still teaching that the English were terrible people who had conquered our country and tried to crush our faith. So I grew up just like any sort of pro-I.R.A. bloke. Talk about indoctrination! The Irish priests and nuns could have given Hitler's chaps a few wrinkles in brain-washing.

It was only much later, when I came over to ride in England, that I realised how narrow and bigoted this attitude was. I grew to love the country. I liked riding on English courses, and was thrilled with the way I was treated and accepted. Later on this realisation was to have a big influence on my rehabilitation, particularly at the start.

I think that in Ireland you had a lot of religion drummed into you—but not a lot of Christianity. Not enough emphasis was placed on human nature, on its strengths, failings and weaknesses. Your character and outlook were formed by the Church. After all, the Jesuits have always claimed: 'Give me a boy until he's seven and he's mine for life.' Possibly because I was never subject to one lot of priests or nuns for any length of time, they didn't succeed with me.

Strangely it was my father, the great jockey, who was the more religious of my parents, and who wielded the greater influence by insisting on the puritanical religious outlook. He was always making us say the Rosary.

My mother was different. She was twenty years younger than my father, whom she married while he was living at Newmarket as a jockey. She was only nineteen when they were wed and she had no racing background at all. She was—and happily still is—a lovely woman, as beautiful as her sister, the film-star Valerie Hobson, who married the charming ill-starred English politician, John Profumo. To judge from the way that his career was shaping when, as a Cabinet Minister, he had to resign in the famous Profumo call-girl case, I suppose that I could well have had Britain's Prime Minister as my uncle by marriage. This just might have straightened out all the mix-up. But the thought of Bobby Beasley getting plastered at No. 10 Downing Street is not altogether un-funny!

So, although both my parents were Catholics, it was my mother who did her best to help me break out of the puritannical strait-jacket. Perhaps because she was so much younger, she had a liberal outlook. She knew that I had been too sheltered and she tried to persuade me to go out, mix with people and get to know girls—in other words to start a normal sort of adolescence. But father's influence was too strong.

Finally they sent me to Newbridge College, where I did quite well academically. At that stage I imagined that I was going to the university to take an agricultural degree and become a farmer. Although he never said much, I believe this is what father wanted me to do. I was big for my age and loved rugby football. By the time I was fourteen I was playing front-row forward in the college team.

I left school the same year, an Irish boy about to be launched into life about which I was totally ignorant, terrified of girls, frightened even of myself. Remember, this was the same age at which my poor brother was 'damned' for masturbation which is now accepted in more enlightened circles as a normal, healthy part of growing up. Even today, however, some of the older clergy in Ireland refuse to recognise it as anything but a terrible sin. And, although I had left school, the 'Emerald Church' had not finished with me by a long way.

It was strange how the sudden change happened. Certainly, my father's life had been all racing. He had retired from the saddle as his sight began to go. At this time he was training about ninety horses at Maddenstown on the Curragh. Most of them belonged to that extraordinary woman, Dorothy Paget, and the licence was held by Charlie Rogers, whom she called 'Romeo', although father did all the training. I shall never forget the day when, in order to assert his authority, Charlie Rogers deliberately humiliated my father, giving him an appalling rocket for something trivial, in front of his own stable-lads and me. As though there weren't enough chips on my young shoulders! That incident bred a fierce resentment of authority which never mellowed until I got to England.

My father was a sick man, although I didn't realise it at the time. The good old days were almost over. No more Monte Carlo for him. He was taking to the booze, but it wasn't until he was dying that I realised why. He never in any way pushed me towards horses. I was big and bound to be heavy, so that it was obvious that I would never be able to ride on the Flat, and therefore there was no point in apprenticing me.

So, even surrounded by horses as I had been all my life, I had never shown any real interest. I went racing at the Curragh a few times, but I wasn't keen, and, unlike some of my contemporaries such as Pat Taaffe, I didn't go to the Pony Club, nor did I have any of the hunting background normal for a boy of my upbringing in Ireland.

Perhaps my father felt that racing had, in a way, let him down, and he didn't want me to finish up on the scrapheap when the riding, the glory and the shouting were over. He knew so well that you had to accumulate a lot of money as a safeguard for the future, and I suppose he felt that, as he hadn't been able to make sufficient from all his success on the Flat before his premature retirement, there was little hope for me who would have to ride jumping because of my weight. So he wanted me to gain the necessary qualifications for a responsible job outside racing. It would be important for me, he believed, to have a good education.

Then that summer when I was fourteen, my grandmother came over from England and we started talking about racing. In retrospect I had little chance of resisting her arguments. It was a glorious July and we sat or walked and talked in that house and garden on the Curragh, steeped in racing memories, thronged with the ghosts of horses, jockeys and trainers—that large, flat plain of turf with the racecourse, the gallops and the sheep, surrounded by training stables and stud farms. Until recently the sheep used to roam across the racecourse. But, of course, they 'track'—follow after each other and make paths—when they are unshepherded, and, once the valuable Irish Sweeps Derby was instituted, the Irish Parliament legislated that the course itself might be enclosed.

I think that wide, galloping track with its long, stiff straight, is the finest test of a mile and a half horse in the world—an even fairer circuit than Chantilly, which is also right-handed and very similar in make and shape.

Away on its own at one side of the Curragh is Curragh Camp, where the hated English cavalry regiments were stationed in the early part of the century. Now the Irish Army occupies the camp and, as the washing flutters on the clotheslines outside the married quarters, the whole set-up looks just like a sensationally authentic film-set for a Kipling story.

Newbridge and Kildare are the two towns on either side of the Curragh. Every morning you will see horses working or schooling with far more variety than you seem to find at Newmarket. Everything is dedicated to the horse. Close by is the Irish National Stud at Tully. My father used to tell me how this stud, with its famous Japanese Garden, which we used to enjoy as children, had been given to the British nation in 1915 by Colonel Hall Walker, for the purpose of forming the National Stud. This eccentric, peppery man was a fervent student of the stars and based all his important decisions on whatever they appeared to foretell. To the dismay of his several trainers this governed the running of his horses. Unfortunately the stars advised him to sell Prince Palatine, who proceeded to win the St Leger and two Ascot Gold Cups. However, he bred some splendid horses, including Minoru, winner of the Guineas and the Derby when leased to King Edward VII, and it was he, later created Lord Wavertree, who persuaded the Aga Khan to come into racing. He didn't just give the magnificent stud at Tully, but included in the gift four stallions, forty-five top-class brood-mares, foals, yearlings, hunters, cart-horses and six hundred head of cattle. Also forage and everything which was on the land or in the buildings, including valuable furniture and pictures.

During the Second World War the British and Irish governments mutually agreed on the transfer of the operation to England. So in 1944 the land at Tully became vested in Ireland while all the livestock were shipped to England, where a new National Stud had been established at Gillingham in Dorset. Later, of course, it moved to its present quarters at Newmarket. I believe that move across the Irish Channel with all those animals in wartime was quite a feat. Once the British had gone, Tully was established as the Irish National Stud, which has over the years been of excellent service to the country's breeders.

So, as I say, my grandmother had a lot going for her as we talked that July. She somehow made me realise that racing was a family tradition dating back over a hundred years and that, although my father was training at Maddenstown, here was I, his son, with no interest in the sport at all. She must have been very persuasive. It's hard to explain what happened. When she said: 'Why don't you try it?' I responded. Suddenly that August I decided that I was going to be a jockey. I just wouldn't go back to school. Mother was very good about it. She reckoned that when somebody had made up his mind to do something, you shouldn't try to stop him. I think that perhaps in a sort of quiet way she wanted me to do it. She always has given me great encouragement and she helped me a lot in those early days.

Father encouraged me too. They had both left me to form my own ideas but I think that even they were taken aback by my complete dedication to the new life. They engaged a tutor to try to continue my education. It was quite useless. The man didn't last a week. I paid no attention at all. All the time I thought of nothing but riding. Anything else was a waste of time. Racing was my life and I was going all out for it. I was an absolute slave to it. Moreover I still am a slave to my warped religious environment.

Instead of being a normal healthy teenager, I was growing up with a twisted sort of morality. I was shy of girls, even frightened of them. To think of them was sinful and wicked. So I seldom went out, and any hopes of gaining confidence were rudely shaken at one of the first dances that I went to. I couldn't dance and I was afraid to try. But somehow I summoned up courage and asked a girl to dance with me. I was going round thinking of how to put a few steps together, without kicking my partner on the shins and knocking her down, and I began to think that we were doing pretty well, when suddenly I received a sharp tap on the shoulder. It was a priest. 'You're dancing immorally', he said. 'I want to see six inches between!' Of course at that time I thought I had been doing something wrong. Now, years later, I realise that it was the priest, not I, who had the bad, sick, twisted mind.

Over in England, when I was quite a bit older, I had cause to remember the priest's particular choice of measurements. England's battered, beloved former champion jockey, Jack Dowdeswell, had been taken to hospital after a very heavy fall, but had recovered sufficiently to be drinking gin and tonic in a well-known pub on the way back from the races, when Dave Dick swaggered in. 'How did you get on, Jack?' he asked. For once Jack was embarrassed. He blushed deep red and stammered in his deep bass voice: 'I had to have fifteen stitches in my old man.'

'Fifteen stitches?' shouted Dave in a voice that echoed round the bar, 'You're boasting!'

CHAPTER 3

Tradition

My grandmother had told me to look up the old books, to study the trophies and the pictures around the house, to re-live the great days of the Beasleys.

I took her advice and I was convinced. In fourteen years from 1878 to 1891 the 'amateur' Beasleys, my grandfather and his brothers, won four Grand Nationals, finished second six times and third twice. It is a unique record, unequalled even by those great Welsh brothers, Jack, Owen and Ivor Anthony.

The onslaught started just thirty-nine years after Lottery won the race regarded as the first official Aintree National (the two earlier 'Grand National Steeplechases' were probably run on a course near Maghull). Before the big race in 1878 there was a scare, when blazing straw was found beneath the royal box that had been erected for the Prince of Wales.

Mr Tom Beasley set off at a great gallop on the Irish entry Martha and was only overhauled inside the last furlong by Shifnal, who beat the mare by two lengths. Tom was unlucky. He lodged an official protest for foul riding against the winning jockey, Jack Jones, and this was the first time that an objection had been heard against a National winner.

It was obviously considered very bad form and was quickly overruled by the stewards.

The following year four of the eighteen riders who weighed out for the National were Beasleys. Tom had been booked for Martha again, Willie rode Lord Marcus, John was on Victor II and my grandfather Harry, on Turco.

Once more Tom tried to make all the running, but, although Martha jumped as well as ever, she failed to stay the $4\frac{1}{2}$-mile course (according to *Ruff's Guide* it was not altered to its present distance of 4 miles 856 yards until 1907) and finished third behind another Irish candidate, The Liberator, owned and ridden by Garrett Moore. On this, their first experience of the formidable Aintree fences, both Harry and Willie completed the course.

Many of those who justifiably admire Vincent O'Brien's amazing feat of saddling three consecutive Grand National winners, Early Mist (1953), Royal Tan (1954) and Quare Times (1955), are apt to forget that another great Irish trainer, H. E. Linde, so nearly achieved the hat-trick more than seventy years earlier.

At Eyrefield Lodge on the Curragh, Linde, backed by patient owners, trained good young horses with just one objective, to win the National. On his Curragh schooling grounds he built actual duplicates of the Aintree fences and, helped by the Beasley brothers, he made sure that his horses were foot perfect, and trained to the minute, when they arrived at Liverpool. Their success there—and in so many big races on other courses in England, Ireland and France during their preparation—was so great, that an English writer lamented: 'We have beyond all doubt lost the supremacy in the rearing and preparation of cross-country performers.'

But Empress, whom Linde produced in 1880, was only a novice in the eyes of the English public. They knew that she was only a five-year-old who had been lightly raced on the Flat, and they backed their old favourites, The Liberator and ten-year-old Regal, who, in 1876, had been the third winner in four years for Newmarket's famous owner-trainer, Captain Machell. The Irish, on the other hand, knew of Empress' tough preparation, how ruthlessly she had been schooled, and how highly she had been tried. They supported their knowledge with confidence, particularly since Mr Tom Beasley was to ride the big chesnut mare. She was named after the Empress of Austria, who often visited Linde while on hunting holidays in Ireland. Grandfather rode Woodbrook for the stable, and Uncle John was on Victoria.

The Prince of Wales and a record crowd saw all three brothers complete the course. Tom rode a confident race, bringing Empress with a steady run from Valentine's Brook to ping the last (they had two hurdles in the straight in those days) and beat The Liberator by two lengths.

Woodbrook finished fifth and, recognising that nothing succeeds like success, Linde put Tom on Woodbrook in 1881, when the ground was a quagmire and the shrewd Curragh trainer knew that conditions were ideally suited to his seven-year-old mudlark. It must have been a gruelling contest. Apart from the obstacles, the runners had also to negotiate plough and root fields. No wonder some of the thirteen starters could barely raise a trot after three miles. Old Regal battled gallantly to the last hurdle, but Uncle Tom and Woodbrook pulled away from him with ease to win in a canter by four lengths, once again heavily supported at 6 to 1.

The next year should have seen a hat-trick for Tom, with Linde-trained horses filling the first two places. It's always surprising, considering the transport difficulties, how far they travelled their horses a hundred years ago. The Linde-Beasley partnership had already landed not only the Conyngham Cup at Punchestown, but the Paris Hurdle in France, with an outstanding young horse called Seaman. However, the six-year-old, undergoing the usual Linde preparation, failed to satisfy his trainer that he was sound enough to win the National. Certainly he had the necessary speed and stamina, but he was lame behind. Like so many Irish trainers before and since, even Linde had an Achilles heel. He was too greedy and too much of a dealer. So he patched Seaman up, and offered him for sale, hoping to catch a 'mug'. He thought he succeeded when a young Guards officer, Lord Manners, bought the horse for £2,000 and sent him to be trained by James Jewett at Newmarket.

Conditions at Liverpool were nearly as bad as the previous year. Tom Beasley was on the well-tried and heavily-backed Linde five-year-old Cyrus, owned by John Gubbins, the former owner of Seaman. Grandfather rode the stable's other runner, Mohican, who was equally fancied, and Lord Manners took the mount on his new purchase.

Mohican fell, but it looked all over for Linde and Tom as Cyrus galloped strongly into the lead as they met the hurdles. Perhaps he was too confident. It happens to the best of us from time to time and he was certainly blamed for it afterwards. What Tom didn't know as he was coming home for his third successive Grand National victory, was that the stable's brilliant cast-off, Seaman, who could have been his mount, had stayed sound enough to finish the course. Despite the inexperience of his young rider, the brilliant speed which had triumphed at Auteuil enabled him to close with his former stable-companion up the straight. Although he screwed over the last hurdle a length behind, he just managed to get up on the run-in and win by a head, to tumultuous English cheers.

'Bell's Life' wrote that Beasley 'rode in a hustled manner, which suggested he had been caught unawares'.

But as Seaman hobbled back to the winners' enclosure, so hopelessly broken down behind that he would surely never race again, it was clear that the mortified Linde had been right in his diagnosis, if not in his precipitate greedy action when advising his owner to sell.

There was more heavy going in 1883, when Tom rode the favourite Zitella, with whom he had earlier won at Kempton, and my grandfather was again on Mohican. It appears that Linde's preparation may have been too rigorous for both horses, even though Zitella did manage to scramble into the third place behind Zoedone, ridden by her Austrian owner, Count Charles Kinsky, one of the most popular of all those great Corinthians.

My grandfather was probably unlucky not to win for Linde the next year. He rode Frigate, and Uncle Tom was on Cyrus, the runner-up two years earlier. Frigate, now a six-year-old, was destined to compete in seven Nationals, finishing second three times before she eventually triumphed. It shows you how much nonsense is talked about a 'Liverpool type of horse'— you know, the massive, powerful sort of chaser with an enormous backside, who, in the words of that great jumping enthusiast, the late Lord Bicester, 'Walks as though he has just shat himself'.

The Hon. George Lambton, a highly successful amateur rider, was a great friend of my grandfather and his brothers. In his wonderful book, *Men and Horses I Have Known*, he described Frigate when he, himself, had his first ride in the National. He wrote:

> Frigate, who had hailed from the celebrated Eyrefield establishment in Ireland, was trained by H. E. Linde, a man who turned out many great steeplechase winners. A little mare, barely 15.3, all wire and whipcord, without an ounce of superfluous flesh on her, who was not much to look at, but no man could have built a more truly made one and when that great jockey, Harry Beasley, threw his leg across her, she looked what she was, a mass of vitality and gameness.

Now, with memories of Battleship, Kilmore, Team Spirit and my own National winner, Nicolaus Silver, we can look back and laugh. There is no doubt in my mind that the smaller, quality thoroughbred is just as well equipped to make a leading steeplechaser as the lumbering giant, who is, fortunately in my opinion, becoming an anachronism as the Irish draught mare fades away.

Now Voluptuary was one of the modern sort. Like Frigate, only more so. He was bred at the Hampton Court Stud and was originally owned by Queen Victoria. Offered for sale, he was bought for 660 guineas by Lord Rosebery, later to become the only man ever to win the Derby while in office as Prime Minister of Britain. (Incidentally I knew a dear old man, who liked to be thought a lot younger than he was to further his success with the girls. But, after a good win on the Derby, his father had christened him Ladas, so that he was labelled for life: 'born 1894!').

Voluptuary showed sufficient class on the Flat to be saddled for the Derby of 1881, but he was no great shakes, and two years later was sold to Mrs H. F. Boyd at the Newmarket Sales for 150 guineas. He remains to this day one of the best-bred horses ever to win a National—he was by the 1872 Derby winner Cremorne out of Miss Evelyn—and must have been a wonderful bargain in any case. Over obstacles he had won just two hurdle races and had never jumped a fence in public. Strange credentials for a National horse. On the other hand he had been hunted so often in Warwickshire since his purchase, that people said he had jumped every fence in the county. And those Warwickshire fences have always been big. About three weeks before Aintree, Voluptuary, partnered by his big race jockey, Ted Wilson, impressed in a mixed gallop with top-class horses at Upton, in which George Lambton rode.

At this time all the jumping jockeys rode 'long'—with long stirrup leathers and what can best be described today as a hunting seat. Mr E. P. 'Ted' Wilson, a short-legged man, with immensely powerful back and shoulders, was the exception.

Lambton says:

> Although we had no doubt as to his great ability in the saddle, to our idea he had a very ugly seat, for he rode

with short stirrups and took a short hold of his reins. In fact he was the first man I ever saw who rode somewhat after the fashion of the present day.

Mind, Lambton was writing fifty years ago. Despite his ugly seat, Ted Wilson won the National in successive years on Voluptuary and Roquefort.

In 1884, the first of these occasions, he arrived at Liverpool, fully confident that Voluptuary was the best horse in the race, even though the fifteen-horse field included such good chasers as Zoedone, Frigate (Mr H. Beasley), Roquefort, Zitella (Mr W. Beasley), Cyrus (Mr T. Beasley), Satellite, and Regal, who was now well past his best. This was the first time that the Prince of Wales had a starter in the race, but, although The Scot gave him a good run for his money, he lost his chance at Becher's second time round.

Coming to the hurdles, Zoedone led from Roquefort and Frigate. But Count Kinsky's brave mare had 12 st 2 lb instead of last year's 11 st, and the going was right on top. Coming to the last, my grandfather drove Frigate to the front and appeared to have won his battle with Roquefort and Voluptuary. But his mare stumbled badly on landing and Ted Wilson's mount, producing his Flat speed, came away to win by four lengths.

According to Lambton, the winning owner was, in fact, none other than Arthur Cooper, 'the clever little man who had so much to do with Fred Archer, a straight fellow and a big gambler'. They brought off a really big coup, and they repeated the performance the following year. Says Lambton:

> Arthur Cooper won a big stake on Voluptuary and Ted Wilson told me that he himself won enough money to pay all his debts and start afresh. Voluptuary was a brilliant horse, but he was greatly helped to victory by the ground, which was on the hard side. Had the going been heavy, there might have been another story.

On the strength of this success Wilson, most impressed by the running of Roquefort, who had finished third only six lengths behind Frigate, persuaded Arthur Cooper to buy this splendid, short-legged half-brother to the St Leger runner-up Miguel, by Winslow out of Cream Cheese. Cooper engineered the coup, and won another small fortune for himself, while Ted Wilson this time set himself up for life.

It was 1885, when for the first time the race was run entirely on grass, and the whole of the Aintree course was railed in. Roquefort was hot favourite at 100 to 30. He had only 11 st to carry, getting 10 lb from my grandfather's mount Frigate, and 11 lb from the top-weight Zoedone.

It is terrifying how much harm has been done to racing by bookmakers. God knows why we still have them in England and Ireland. They suck the blood of the sport, which provides them with a means of making a fat living. Through them a jockey's life can become purgatory. Later on I'll tell the story of how I was offered twelve times as much to stop the favourite in a great race, than I received for winning it. But, as at the age of fourteen, I read the horrifying details of the Grand National of 1885, I never dreamed that my fate and that of Nicolaus Silver—on the same course in the same race seventy-six years later—could so easily have been the same as that of Count Charles Kinsky and his beloved mare Zoedone.

The 1883 winner, now still only eight years old, was, according to Lambton, who completed the course on Lioness, 'the safest fencer in the world'. Zoedone, a sound second favourite, had been coupled in many Spring Doubles with that fine horse Bendigo, who had just won the Lincolnshire Handicap, and bookmakers stood to lose heavily if she won.

At this time horses still had to jump a preliminary hurdle on the way to the start, but this was just a formality for the mare who loved jumping and racing. Now, however, Zoedone blundered into it and fell heavily. Charles Kinsky, who loved the English as much as they loved him, could never believe that anyone could have done anything to hurt him and Zoedone.

He remounted and made his way quietly to the start. But, as soon as they jumped off, he realised that his mare was not a shadow of her normal self. He said later that she had none of her usual zest, but was just jumping from memory, following the others round the course. When she came to Becher's for the second time, this brave extravagant jumper suddenly spiralled into the air and crashed with a twisted, convulsive fall, writhing and thrashing about in terrible pain. A huge, angry crowd of those standing by the famous fence and on the railway embankment surged forward to look at the stricken mare. But when they saw the face of her owner, they drew back. A woman said: 'None of us will ever forget the way Count Kinsky looked. Everyone knew how he loved that mare.' Eighty years on I was to think back to that early case of criminal doping, when favourites I rode myself were got at and I gave evidence for the prosecution in the subsequent trial of the nobblers.

Then, as a sheltered, frustrated boy, I was learning that I was direct heir to a thrilling, glamorous, heady life of danger, glory and sportsmanship. This was my own grandfather and his brothers who were referred to as 'great', as they won race after race at courses whose names were legendary, like Auteuil, Punchestown, Cheltenham and, of course, Liverpool. I, who had been starved of romance in my priest-ridden puritanical upbringing, was now discovering the excitement and adventure which other boys found in Westerns or tales of King Arthur's Knights, here in my own family. What's more I had the chance of joining that wonderful life, of carrying on the Beasley torch. I was immersed in that romantic past right up to the neck.

In my mind I stood with Charles Kinsky beside the most famous fence in the world looking down at that dear, gallant suffering mare, scarcely heeding now the rest of the National, in which Grandfather and little Frigate put up a tremendous performance, only to be beaten two lengths by Roquefort.

The veterinary report showed that Zoedone had indeed been poisoned and the Count retired her from racing. She had done him so well. Always a fine horseman and, even in those days, outstandingly brave in the hunting field, he became, after his Aintree success, a very fine cross-country rider, winning numerous races.

Like many of his Corinthian friends, he was also a bold and fearless gambler. I was fascinated by the way they won and lost thousands of pounds and thought how much those sums represented at the time. Count Kinsky graced the English social and sporting scene for many years. He always spent more than half the year in England. Lambton wrote:

> I said good-bye to him at the end of Goodwood week in July 1914, when he left to go and fight for his own country, and on the side of the Germans, a nation he had always hated.
>
> He volunteered for service on the Russian front so that he should avoid having to fight against the English and the French, and for two years he was with the Austrian Cavalry at the age of fifty-eight, or more.
>
> He died in 1919, and if ever a man died of a broken heart, Charles Kinsky did. His own country ruined and done for, and he himself debarred from coming to the country he loved and where his friends were.

So hard did he ride out hunting, that on one day with the Quorn a whipper-in, who had seen him fall, reported that the Count had been killed. As at that moment hounds set off again in full cry, even his dearest friends found they could not stop to investigate! But when Kinsky, bloody but unbowed, turned up at the end of the hunt, one of them asked the whip: 'What the devil do you mean by telling us the Count was killed?' To which the hunt servant answered: 'Well, if he ain't dead now, by God he soon will be!'

Twenty-three runners started for the National of 1886, a big field for those days. Grandfather was once again on Frigate and Uncle Tom rode Linde's other entry, Too Good. Such was the magnetism of the trainer-jockey combination that Too Good was backed down to 7 to 1 despite having a suspect leg.

Horses should never be given names like that. It's tempting providence, asking for trouble. For instance Winagain never won, and Passifyoucan was always being passed. So, after a scramble for the first fence, in which Frigate was brought down, Too Good just wasn't good enough to defeat the powerful ex-harness horse and hunter, Old Joe, who had once changed hands for only £30.

The next year was a bad one for Linde and the three Beasley brothers, although they set off with high hopes. Three fancied runners from the stable featured in the sixteen starters. Frigate, Too Good, and Spahi, a typical Linde candidate, a really good winner on the Flat, but never having run in public over hurdles or fences. For once, however, the Eyrefield Lodge schooling grounds had not worked the oracle. Spahi fell at the third fence, and the race was won by Gamecock from Zoedone's half-brother Savoyard, who had been considered unlucky when falling at the last the previous year.

The following day, Spahi demonstrated what a good thing he could have been in the National. Saddled by Linde for a two-mile flat race, he was only just beaten by Bird of Freedom, who went on to win the Ascot Gold Cup!

Another Linde-Beasley 'certainty', the brilliant, unbeaten Usna, who was carrying top-weight of 12 st 7 lb, came to grief second time round the following year—1888—when the hurdles in the straight were replaced by two fences inside the Flat course. The stable's other two runners were Spahi, and Frigate, ridden on this occasion by my great-uncle Willie, who had nearly always been there, but had not yet finished in the frame.

What a fascinating sport it is! Suddenly out of the blue appears a totally unknown jockey who has his moment of glory, and then vanishes from the record book just as suddenly. Such a jockey was Mawson, who won the 1888 National on Playfair, whose only claim to a place in the Aintree field was victory in

44

a hurdle race at Sandown. Poor Mawson. He was never even given an initial, let alone a Christian name. Just Mawson.

And he owed his success to one of those gestures for which steeplechasing has always been renowned. He had no chance second time round when Playfair straddled a big fence and had his jockey almost off, clinging round his neck. But Arthur Nightingall, who was about to become one of the great Liverpool jockeys, now close behind on The Badger, reached forward and pulled him back on to the saddle.

It was in 1938 that a similar incident occurred, which also ended in victory. This time the 'angel' was Fred Rimell, champion jockey before and after the war, who was later to provide me with my own National winner.

Seventeen-year-old Bruce Hobbs was soaring over the tricky fence after Bechers, on Battleship. A length behind came Fred, riding Provocative. The little American chesnut stallion pitched badly on landing, shooting his tall, gangling young rider over his shoulder. 'I was completely gone,' says Bruce. 'I had no chance!' He had indeed reached the point of no return when help came from an unexpected quarter. Fred says, 'I shouted, "Where do you think you're going, mate?" seized him by the seat of his pants and yanked him back into the saddle. He went on and won a thrilling race. Me, I fell at the Canal Turn—the very next fence!'

In this 1888 National George Lambton rode Savoyard, a most unlucky horse, who was knocked over when winning the Paris Steeplechase, fell at the last hurdle of the National, and should have won in 1887 if Tom Skelton, broke as ever, had not had a rush of blood and come too soon. He was a real Liverpool horse and a perfect ride over big fences. He had a big weight, 12 st 4 lb, but he was very much fancied.

To give the best idea of the atmosphere which my boy brain was now absorbing, I will quote the eye-witness account of that race from the pen of Savoyard's jockey, who rode the winners of the National Hunt at Cheltenham, and the Paris Steeplechase the same year:

An Irish horse called Usna was favourite. He was a smashing good horse, trained by Linde, and ridden by Harry Beasley. He carried top weight, 12 st 7 lb. In the field was the Irish mare, Frigate, who had been second to Roquefort in 1885, very much fancied, ridden by another of the Beasley brothers, Willie. In the race, after we had gone a mile, Usna, in spite of his 12 st 7 lb, went to the front, followed by Frigate, and so great was the pace that, as we passed the stands the first time round, these two had already strung out the field, one of the few who was able to keep anywhere near being myself on Savoyard. Coming to the fence at the Canal Turn, they were quite ten lengths in front of me: on landing over this fence Usna put his shoulder out. He did not fall, but he carried Frigate out almost to the brink of the canal. But for this unfortunate accident I have no doubt that Usna and Frigate would have beaten the rest of the field nearly a quarter of a mile. Up to the moment I had been obliged to keep my horse at full stretch to remain near them, but when they ran out the situation altered. Savoyard went with his head in his chest, jumping like a bird, and the others struggled after me.

This was the first year that the race was run over the present National course, finishing over those two small fences inside the flat race-course: previously, we had always finished up the flat race-course with two flights of hurdles to end up. That year these two new fences were built, much too straight up and were as strong as a wall. As we came on to the race-course, Ringlet, a mare in Captain Machell's stable, and ridden by Tom Skelton, passed me, but approaching the first of these new fences she was beaten and my nearest pursuer was Playfair, the ultimate winner: he was quite four lengths behind me and Mawson had his whip up. It went through me then that I was going to win the National if I got safely over the last fences. Now Savoyard was never so good over

46

the small fences as big ones, and I did the most fatal
thing a jockey can do at the end of a long steeplechase.
Coming to the fence I steadied my horse, he got a little
too close to it, just brushed the top and turned over like
a rabbit shot through the head. Playfair went on to win
easily from Frigate, who had made up an extraordinary
amount of ground, after being carried out (she won the
National the following year). When I had picked myself
up I first thought of the advice Captain Machell had once
given me. He said that at the end of a long steeplechase,
even if winning easily, a jockey should never let his horse
down but drive him at his last fences.

There were two stories told about me over this fall,
which were amusing and both equally untrue. In my fall
I lost my whip which I was very fond of, and I kept
walking round and round looking for it. Not finding it,
I walked back to the fence, thinking I might have dropped
it when my horse hit the fence, for he fell some lengths
beyond it. Garrett Moore, who was always the first man
to go and pick up a fallen jockey, or do any other good-
natured action, thought that I had got concussion from
the way I was walking round. Instead of that he found
that I was not in the least hurt, but only looking for my
whip, and on our way home we came across it, thrown an
almost incredible distance from where I had fallen. My
brother Durham, who was on the stand, declared that I
was walking to the canal to throw myself in, and that
Garrett Moore had saved me from suicide. The other
story was that dear old Jenkins, who trained Savoyard,
many times told people that I had lost my head, and
driven the horse wildly at the fence. I wish I had, all
would then have been well.

In 1889 Frigate finally justified persistence. There is no
doubt that a true National horse will keep coming back for
more on the course. Bryan Marshall, one of the finest Aintree

riders of recent years, used to say that for that course you want a horse with no imagination, that will never shy at things in the hedge, a bold horse, probably a stupid horse. But so many keep getting round and running into a place without ever winning.

Frigate's owner-breeder, Mr M. A. Maher, had sold her, but bought her back. The three times she had been second had been in his colours. In his book *A Hundred Grand Nationals*, T. H. Bird described her as 'the best mare that has ever won the Grand National'. Tom Beasley had the ride this year and, after seeing Voluptuary and Roquefort fall, he drove her on with all his superb strength and balance to beat the newcomer Why Not by a length, at odds of 8 to 1. The cheers, which were loud enough to be heard in Manchester, testified to the popularity of the mare and her rider, who was winning his third National.

It's hard to know which records to believe. Some say that it was in this year that the distance was established at $4\frac{1}{2}$ miles and, from my researches, I am inclined to support this view and disagree with that of Ruff's Guide, which insists that the great chase was not run over 4 miles 856 yards until 1907.

As far as I was concerned, however, it was another great day for the Irish—and, in particular, for the Beasleys.

I read on—to 1890 where Frigate slipped at the fence before Valentine's and Ilex, a hunter-chaser, ridden by Arthur Nightingall and heavily backed down to 4 to 1 favouritism, beat the 100 to 1 chance Pan, described by George Lambton, who had been closely associated with him as 'the biggest rogue that ever was'.

So we came to the great Grand National of 1891, for which the 4 to 1 favourite was seven-year-old Come Away, trained and ridden by my grandfather, Harry Beasley. He was the only jockey who had ever ridden the horse, on whom he had already won races at Punchestown and Liverpool. Grandfather knew all too well that Come Away had suffered trouble with a suspensory ligament since his four-year-old days.

Uncle Tom Beasley, having his last National ride on the

Linde-trained Cruiser, was well backed. Former winners, Voluptuary, Roquefort and Gamecock were making their final attempts, and last year's hero, Ilex, was also in the line-up. Add to this the 1889 runner-up Why Not, and a newcomer, Cloister, ridden by the fanatical soldier-amateur Roddy Owen, who had dedicated himself to the job of winning the National. The elder Owen brother Hugh, one of the best men to hounds in England and a fair jockey, had been killed, as he would have wanted, jumping a fence in Leicestershire.

Captain Roddy Owen was a steeplechase rider of the highest order, who had vowed that he would give up racing and take soldiering seriously once he had won the National. He always went the shortest way and was not too particular how he got there. His reactions were lightning and he would take advantage of anything or anyone in a race.

Although he was a most attractive man, an officer and an amateur, he was like Lester Piggott in that there was nothing he would not do to get the ride on any horse he fancied. Not unnaturally he was, for a while, somewhat unpopular with the professional jockeys—'taking the bread and butter out of their mouths'—and one day at Sandown they said they would sort him out and get a bit of their own back. Lambton says:

> After a race that was rather like a Rugby football match, Roddy emerged from the scrum and won. I went into the weighing-room afterwards and found them all laughing and the best of friends, saying that they would not take the Captain on again at the rough game, as he could beat the lot at it. Whatever he did, no one could quarrel with Roddy for long.

He was very popular in his regiment with both officers and men. And it was a strange coincidence that so many years later I was to win the Cheltenham Gold Cup on the horse named after him. However, the gallant Captain found that the Beasley

49

legend was no myth when he took on my grandfather in the National.

Once again let George Lambton, the eye-witness, who was hoping for the success of his old friend Charlie Cunningham on Why Not, tell the tale:

The National of that year was an extraordinarily interesting race. In the field there were no less than four previous winners. Roquefort, Ilex, Gamecock, and Voluptuary, added to these Why Not, who had been second to Frigate, and the great raking Cloister, who had already shown that he was a typical Liverpool horse. The favourite was Come Away, an Irish horse, who had been carrying all before him, and was said by the Irish division to be 'walking over'. He had the redoubtable Harry Beasley for his jockey. Cloister all his life had suffered from indifferent jockeyship, but now he was to be ridden by Roddy Owen. Trained by Dick Marsh, he had done a splendid preparation, and Newmarket was full of confidence. There was one fly in the ointment, Roddy had hurt his leg, so that he was not able to do the hard work necessary for him to be quite at his best, for, like so many horses, he himself wanted a strenuous preparation.

Come Away, Ilex, Why Not, and Cruiser, who was ridden by Tommy Beasley, had not been seen in public that year, and yet they were the four best backed horses in the race, and six furlongs from home they were all in the fight. Come Away was the property of a young Irishman, Willie Jameson. He and his two brothers were less known in the racing world than in other realms of sport, such as big game shooting, fishing, hunting and yachting. Willie himself was a famous yachtsman, and I believe was as good at that game as his jockey, Harry Beasley, was over fences. He sailed the Prince of Wales' Britannia in many of her famous races. I once had the good luck to be with him on one of these occasions, when he completely 'out-jockeyed', or whatever the nautical term may be, his opponents.

Now Come Away was a really magnificent bay horse, and his looks and condition thoroughly justified his favouritism, yet it was no secret that he had a leg which had been causing considerable trouble.

Why Not looked a picture, and filled the eye more than he had ever done before. Ilex, Gamecock, Cruiser, Roquefort, any of them looked good enough to win, but the latter had not his old pilot, E. P. Wilson. What occurred in the early stages of the race I cannot quite remember, but my impression is that Why Not was always more or less in front. Anyhow, about five furlongs from home, Why Not on the inside, Cloister next to him, and Come Away on the outside, were racing together. So well was Why Not going that it really looked as if Charlie was at last going to bring it off, but coming to the last fence Roddy did not give him too much room, and Why Not came down a fearful crash, he himself being badly hurt. This left Come Away just in the lead, with Cloister creeping up on the inside. Harry Beasley, fearing that his horse's leg would give way, rode very tenderly. A hundred yards from home Roddy drove his horse up to Come Away's girth, but now it was his turn to be squeezed for room, and he could not improve his position, the favourite getting home cleverly by half a length. After the race Roddy lodged an objection, but it was overruled, and I think rightly.

Charles Greenwood, of the *Daily Telegraph*, that best of racing journalists, described the finish of the race most aptly. 'Harry had the Captain in the same position as a man with a cork half-way in the neck of a bottle: one little push and it will go down.' I am sure Harry Beasley will forgive me for saying it, but if it had been needful that push would have been given.

After the race, before the objection was gone into, there

was the deuce of a row in the weighing room: the excited Irish Division surrounding Roddy, declaring they would have his blood. I can see him now, with his back to the wall, cool as a cucumber, saying: 'All right, but wait till it's settled, then I will fight every one of you, single handed or the whole lot of you together.' But hot as the blood was for the moment, there was no ill-feeling left by the next day.

Captain Roddy Owen achieved his ambition the following year by winning on Father O'Flynn. He immediately returned to London and asked the War Office to send him abroad. Following service in various foreign climes, he ended up with Kitchener in Egypt, where four years after his Liverpool triumph, he died of some middle-eastern disease.

My grandfather had his final National ride that year, and so at last the incredible Beasley Liverpool saga was over.

I made little sense during those days as I read and read, living in another world. But my father and mother were very patient with me.

Think of someone like the Hon. George Lambton saying: 'I was so frightened of Harry Beasley, that I dare not pick up my whip', and declaring proudly that when he beat Harry in the Champion at Aintree, it gave him more pleasure than any other race in his life.

Would I ever be like my grandfather?

I then read of all the exploits of my father and Uncle Rufus, their classic successes and the great trainers they had ridden for. Probably because I knew that my weight would always prevent me from taking part, the Flat held very little attraction for me.

But I was sold for ever on the jumping game. My fate was sealed.

CHAPTER 4

Dedication

Once I'd made up my mind, there was no holding me. I became a sort of fanatic. I started on the hacks, of which you always have several in a big training establishment—for the trainer, headman, visitors and for teaching apprentices to ride. Cobs and ponies of different sizes.

The other day I talked to Pat Taaffe about this period of my life. Six years older, he was also on the Curragh, but riding successfully on the Flat, combining it with hurdles and fences when he realised he was going to be too heavy to stay on the level. He was a bit of an all-rounder at this time. Pat said: 'We all thought you were mad. There you were, riding out three, four, five lots a day and, when you couldn't get on a racehorse, you got back on to your pony.'

He's right, of course. I was mad in a way. Mad to make up for the lost years and to become a great jockey like my grandfather. Now that I'd woken up to my heritage, I found that everyone knew about him. He was, and still is, the great legend of the Irish turf. Harry Beasley, the grandest old man of all, who rode his last winner when he was eighty-three years old at the Curragh! He won over Punchestown's tough obstacles at seventy-two.

My father never pushed me. He was an introvert and we didn't have much communication. He guided me along, taught me how to ride, showed me the rudiments and occasionally passed on some hints. He gave me a sort of passive encouragement when I used to ask him how I was doing, but he appeared to have little idea how to express himself about things. I suppose I must have inherited the Beasley touch—there must have been a spark there, because, once I'd decided to start riding and tried to learn as quickly as possible, it all seemed to come easily and naturally.

Most of the ninety horses in the yard belonged to Dorothy Paget, the fabulous patron of National Hunt racing in particular, who became a legend in her own lifetime through her dress—that famous, ever-lasting old grey tweed coat—and her constant entourage of secretaries, her immense appetite, her habit of living at night and her rudeness, which probably stemmed from shyness. I used to hear the stories of how she would lock herself in the lavatory at a race-meeting until all the people had left. Then she would emerge to eat a dinner as large as those Henry VIII enjoyed, firing questions at her trainer and attendants the while.

I never met her, but I was delighted to have learned to ride on her horses. There were two-year-olds being prepared to go to England to be trained by Fulke Walwyn and his twin-sister, Helen Johnson-Houghton. Lovely, all-quality animals, but not much good to me, because I knew I would be too heavy. Still, I'd ride one of them out, if there was nothing else.

But the ones I concentrated on were the 'bumper' horses. These were the young potential high-class National Hunt horses being trained to prove themselves worthy of joining 'D.P's' string of great jumpers with Fulke Walwyn at Saxon House, Upper Lambourn.

'Bumper' is the word used in racing to describe an amateur rider. This is because amateurs, less strong in the leg, fit and

54

practised than professional riders, are inclined to bump the
saddle when they are galloping. The last race of the day at
most Irish meetings is usually a 'bumper', a contest for older
horses that, either at starting or at closing, have not won a
race, to be ridden by amateurs. These are excellent events for
horse and rider and I don't know why they are not included in
English programmes. They provide fun and vital experience for
the jockeys and they not only teach young horses about racing,
but advertise their potential, thereby increasing their value for
sale. Although 'bumpers' are flat races, they are used as the
shop-window for the young, untried Irish-bred hurdlers and
steeplechasers of the future. With a good amateur aboard—
and there are always some pretty good ones in Ireland—a
trainer can sometimes have a decent bet in a bumper too,
But you have to be a bit wary if you're buying and, when the
vendor tells you proudly he won his bumper at ——, just
check up the strength of the race. It may be hard to believe,
but there have been cases when the winner was about the only
trier in the race and the rest of the large field have just been
gaining experience!

Anyway it was the bumper horses that I was concentrating
on, because the only way in Ireland at that time that you could
break into the jumping scene without being first an apprentice
and a Flat jockey was to start as an amateur and then turn
professional. Results show that there's not much wrong with
this method in England either. Recent champion jockeys Stan
Mellor, Terry Biddlecombe, Tim Brookshaw and Dick Francis,
all started their careers and made their names as 'Mister'.

Of course over the years the system has always been abused
to a greater or lesser extent. The amateur has frequently
deserved the description 'shamateur'. Like the late Sandy
Scratchley, who was summoned before the stewards shortly
before the war and asked to produce his bank pass-book for
their inspection. 'As the last entry in it was £100 from Prince
Aly Khan,' said Sandy, 'I decided that discretion was the better
part of valour. So, drawing myself up to my full five feet plus,

I said in as dignified a voice as possible: "Gentlemen, it's been a hard decision. But I've finally made up my mind to turn professional." '

There were various ways of getting round the rules. One very famous soldier-rider, who was as good as the top professionals of his day, would say when asked by the grateful winning owner what he would like as a present: 'A gold cigarette case, please.' He would explain that there was one particular case in the window of a Bond Street jeweller, which he had long coveted. 'In fact,' he said, 'I already had that exact case and, when an owner ordered one for me, the jeweller would just credit me with the cost price and periodically pay me out!'

Back in my grandfather's day, the amateurs were not only very good, but mighty tough mentally and physically as well. Verley Bewicke often tells stories of his uncle Percy Bewicke, the celebrated amateur and highly successful gambler, who was riding at the same time as the Beasley brothers, Roddy Owen, Charles Kinsky, George Lambton and Co.

After he had finished riding, the Captain controlled the Grateley training establishment and engineered enormous coups which took literally hundreds of thousands of pounds out of the Ring. A typical triumph was the plunge on Dumbarton Castle in the Stewards' Cup of 1903. Early the previous season, as a two-year-old, this colt had appeared distinctly useful, but then unaccountably he seemed to lose all his form. He was handicapped at just 7 st 4 lb in the big Goodwood sprint. A week before the Stewards' Cup he was 25 to 1 chance. Then the money started to come in.

On the day, Dumbarton Castle opened at 20 to 1, and, although there were twenty-one runners, he was so heavily backed that he started a hot favourite at 4 to 1. Ridden by the 'job jockey' of the time, Otto Madden, he trotted up and earned more than £60,000 for his connections. Just think what this would be worth today!

Recently Verley, who has trained so successfully in the north and south of England, met an Irish official who saw Uncle Percy win a race at Baldoyle. As the famous amateur rode out of the paddock, he leant down to an old friend and whispered: 'Put me a thousand on this one, Bill.'

It was a tall order to get the equivalent of about £20,000 of today's money on in a weak market just before the 'off'. But Bill did his best, got a decent price and was feeling pleased with himself for having done his old friend, Percy, a good turn when the horse duly obliged and returned to the winners' enclosure. Tight-lipped as ever, the Captain unsaddled with a practised hand and turned to be greeted by his friend. 'Well done, Percy,' said Bill. 'I managed to get 6 to 1, but I'm afraid I could only get £800 on. It was so late and they just wouldn't take any more.' The great amateur stopped and looked at him with undisguised contempt through narrowed eyes. 'That serves me right,' he said. 'I should have known better than to trust a bloody fool like you!'

Many years later Uncle Percy told his great nephew: 'Don't you ever train horses, Verley. There's no money in it these days and it's no longer a gentleman's sport.'

So now there was to be a third Mr H Beasley in direct succession and I couldn't wait to get going. 'How am I shaping up now?' I would ask my father after a morning when I had ridden several gallops. 'You're not doing too badly,' he would say quietly, adding something like: 'I've always found it's better not to ask a horse a question until he's properly balanced and racing under you.' Or maybe he would ask me vaguely: 'Don't you find that you're really sitting in to a horse in a gallop when you've got your elbows outside your knees?' I would mumble yes, never having done it, but, of course, determined to try it the next time I rode fast work. Or again: 'It's getting and keeping your rhythm that counts in a finish' or 'A good jockey can use his whip equally well in either hand and can pull it through so smoothly and quickly that he wouldn't disturb a butterfly', and 'It's just as important a part of the jockey's craft to be able to keep his horse perfectly

balanced galloping on the same leg when he pulls out to make
his challenge as it is to be able to change legs at the gallop
deliberately.'

The day he said that my father thought for a minute or two
in silence. Then, out of the blue he asked me: 'Bobby, did you
ever carry a heavy bucket for some way in your right hand,
then switch it over to the left hand as you were getting tired,
and finally back to the right again?'

He never told me to do this or that or to ride in a certain
way. He would just give me the idea, leaving me to work it
out for myself and practise, practise, practise.

I didn't dare ask him to explain the analogy of the bucket.
He never wasted words and I didn't think he was just romanti-
cising. I worried about it so much and even asked a few experienced people, but they didn't know and I think they thought
I was a bit stupid. It was a long time before I discovered what
my father had been driving at. Even then it was only by
accident. I had been riding in a bumper on a left-handed
course and my horse was naturally galloping on his near foreleg. Although he wasn't fancied I thought as we turned into
the straight that I might have a chance—only a squeak—of
winning. Then, as I kicked, I felt him tiring and he changed
on to his off-fore. I was about to switch him back when my
father's words flashed suddenly through my mind. Was this
what he had meant? I had nothing to lose. So I allowed my
horse to gallop for a short way on the wrong leg. Our two
rivals were pretty tired too and we didn't lose much ground
while I waited. Now! I changed him back on to the near-fore.
Like a giant refreshed he ran on strongly and got up to win
close home. Since then I've used this manoeuvre with great
success on occasions, deliberately changing a horse on to the
wrong leg when tiring and then, after that short rest, switching
him back again. When I've won I've always been grateful to my
father and his buckets.

He tried to hold me back a bit, to stop me from plunging
in before I was ready. But it was no good. Though lacking

experience I was determined to get going, even if I had a lot to do in a short time.

Looking back now, I wish my father had been a tougher character, more commercial, ruthless, even mean. But he loved the game and the game was more important to him than any money. He lived in another era, almost a dream world, where everyone rode to win all the time with no thought of reward except for the honour, the glory and the fun of the sport. If only, instead of instilling this absolute dedication, he could have taught me to be a business man and brought me up with a fairly ruthless, cynical outlook on life, I might not perhaps have been so easily blinded by the glamour and the bright lights later on. It was a pity that I didn't allow Mother with her younger, more liberal outlook to influence me more.

It all seemed to happen in a very short time. My hard work seemed to have paid off and, I suppose, I must have inherited my share of the natural Beasley skills and horse-sense. Less than eighteen months after I started to ride I was competing in my first race.

*   *   *

Blue, yellow hoop on body and sleeves, yellow cap with blue hoop. The many Irish amateur riders who were competing at that time will always associate me in their memories with those famous colours of the late Dorothy Paget. I first put on her silks on January 26, 1952. Once again the name Mr H. Beasley appeared on an Irish racecard. The contest that my father and Charlie Rogers, whom my father was assisting, had chosen for my debut was the Ashford Maiden Flatrace at Leopardstown. It was a humble two-mile affair worth £133 to the winner and there were eighteen starters. My mount was a very moderate four-year-old called Fair Reynard.

Actually on this occasion I was wearing the scarlet cap which signified Dorothy Paget's second colours because our stable had another runner in the same race. This was Touareg, who had shown some ability at home and who was ridden by the experienced, very capable Irish bumper, Pat Hogan. As usual, a fair number of these Irish amateur riders were good, tough horsemen capable of holding their own with the best professional steeplechase jockeys. I was riding against Vincent O'Brien's brother Phonsie, who had been so unlucky not to win the National on Royal Tan, Bunny Cox, Tos Taaffe, brother of the more famous Pat, Pat Hogan, John de Burgh, who had been for some years with Ivor Anthony and is now a leading member of the Turf Club, and so many others. But I must have been a pretty objectionable youth because, looking back, I remember little of those first races and, when I am asked whether I was overawed by these famous men, I have to answer 'No'. It seems that I knew exactly where I was going, and that, with my dedication to racing as the one thing in life, I would soon be much better than them. However, I did learn a lot from those bumper races. They have always been the roughest events of all to ride in because it is a strange part of the Irish character that when competing against each other on horses, nearly everyone wants to 'do' the other riders. They would try to ride each other off, put each other over the rails and so on. If they could give one of their rivals a fall, that was a victory chalked up to them. I knew all about this but, at least to begin with, they didn't try to 'do' me. I suppose they took pity on my age and knew that I was the trainer's son. Little did they know how soon I would be 'doing' them!

On that first occasion both Pat and I finished in the ruck, not in the first eleven. I knew that Fair Reynard would never be any good but I had been able, even at that early stage, to notice how well Touareg was going. Although he ran as green as might have been expected, he was confirming the promise that he had shown on the gallops and I wished that I could be riding him in the future. As soon as I got home after that race I couldn't wait to get going again. More than ever, I would insist on riding out every lot in the morning. Not content with this. I would get out the hacks, the ponies, in the afternoon with my young friend Mick Collins, and we would ride our races together. Poor ponies! We would practise carrying our whips in the right hand then in the left hand, pulling them through in the skilful, accepted way that my father had taught me. A good jockey must learn to do this so smoothly that he does not unbalance his horse. I practised getting more and more stylish. We rode endless finishes and I always won. I beat Mick every time but he came back for more, happy to go on practising with me. Yes, I was quite odious.

Anyhow, my father and Charlie Rogers must have been satisfied with my progress and, as though it had been predestined, my wish came true. Pat Hogan was side-lined after a nasty fall, and on March 15 it was I who rode Touareg in the bumper at Baldoyle. These races vary so much. This one turned out to be a particularly good one. It was won by Paddy Prendergast's Lime Lodge and I was not in the first nine.

A fortnight later I went to Naas to ride Bookhive. This was a rough contest with thirty starters and once again I was not in the first nine behind Friendly Way, ridden by Bunny Cox. Another very hot bumper took place at Phoenix Park ('The Park' as it is called in Ireland) on April 12 when I rode Blue Stream unplaced behind a 20 to 1 outsider, Lord Bicester's newcomer, Mariner's Log, trained by the great Tom Dreaper. Like Dorothy Paget, Lord Bicester was one of the great patrons of National Hunt racing and, although we had no means of knowing it at the time, Mariner's Log was to become a famous jumper.

On May 9 we went back to Leopardstown with Touareg. I suppose they must have thought something of me by now because I was fourth favourite in the Newcastle Maiden Flatrace at 10 to 1. You can really ride a race over that Leopardstown two miles with its stiff uphill finish and it has always been one of my favourite courses. On this occasion I kept Touareg lying handy close up to the leaders until the turn into the straight, where I suddenly found that, although the other riders were clearly uneasy, my horse was going well. We were going better than Bunny Cox, better than Frank Prendergast on Mill Baby and even better than Tos Taaffe on Wild Amy. However Tos was obviously the danger and, thinking of him not as a jockey but as Mick Collins on his pony on the Curragh, I sat down and rode the first strong winning finish of my life. Touareg was returned as the winner by a length from Wild Amy with Mill Baby three lengths away third. Bunny Cox was fifth.

As I rode in acknowledging the cheers and congratulations and my father's shy smile of pride, I felt no real sense of elation. I just knew that from now on I would be the boss in the bumper races, even though I was only sixteen. Racing was the only life, the only job, and it must be done at all costs. I just had to keep trying to win.

Nineteen days later over in England, another boy the same age as myself, who was also the product of a great jumping family, very nearly made racing history. Lester Piggott was just as dedicated as I. But, of course, he had been riding before he could walk. He still reckons that he should have won that Derby in 1952. As it was, he came in for a certain amount of ridicule, which was totally unjustified and was mostly inspired by such quips as 'What did I Tulyar?' and so on.

Scobie Breasley had temporarily returned to Australia. So Lester rode for Druids' Lodge and had the mount on Gay Time in the Derby. Tulyar, the mount of that tough Cockney veteran, Charlie Smirke, was a very good little horse, with that thrilling action possessed by the best. When they are fully extended, they seem to drop about a foot—actually 'getting down to it' and almost justifying the description 'ventre à terre'. But the Aga Khan's colt, whose one two-year-old success had been in the Buggins Farm Nursery at Haydock, was, in Lester's opinion, still short of his best when the Derby came.

Gay Time was the sort of horse that I personally dislike—a large, light chesnut with a flaxen mane and tail—generally signs of softness. He was a grandson of Hyperion and had a distinct look of the great little stallion's son, the Queen's

Aureole, who was now a two-year-old. Both these colts proved the exception to the rule. Although highly strung, they were very game.

Unhappily everything conspired against Gay Time at Epsom. He pulled a plate off in the paddock before the race and, after being replated, had to go down to the start by himself. No picnic for a highly strung thoroughbred in the fairground atmosphere of Epsom Downs on Derby Day. By the time that he had made his way through the shouting crowd down the pathway past the blaring noise of the swings and roundabouts and up the other side to another mass of people thronging the starting gate, he was in a muck lather. He had virtually lost his race already. But 'fear travels down the reins' and, even at that age, Lester, utterly dedicated, passed his confidence to his horse. Moreover Gay Time was made of sterner stuff than his appearance indicated. A slow beginner, he was unable to lay up in the early stages. He was drawn on the outside of a large field of thirty-three runners. As always, those with little chance determined to make a show, galloping as far and as fast as they could up that long pull to the top of Tattenham Hill. When, inevitably, they began to fall back beaten, Lester was forced to come wide, thereby losing a lot of valuable ground.

Rounding Tattenham Corner into the straight, Smirke sent Tulyar into the lead, but now Gay Time slipped into top gear and, galloping on resolutely, began to make up ground and overhaul the little bay. How close he would have got, is anyone's guess. Lester is convinced he would have won if Tulyar had not come across him below the distance and checked him before going on to win by three-quarters of a length. Lester determined to object. Knowing the attitude of the hierarchy to the young star, it is most unlikely that his complaint would have been entertained and the Aga Khan's colt disqualified. In the event, how happy they must have been. The boy jockey was tired. Gay Time, a big, heavy colt, was weary and sprawling. The pull-up at Epsom was the worst in the world.

Lester says: 'As I tried to pull him up, Gay Time collided with the rails, fell over on his head, throwing me off, and then galloped away into the wood behind the paddock. When he was eventually found and I arrived back at the weighing-room to weigh in, lots of people said I had grounds for objection. So I told the Clerk of the Scales that I wanted to lodge an official objection to the winner for crossing and taking my ground.' The Clerk of the Scales looked at him and said bluntly: 'You're too late to object!'

This was the Derby. Even in 1952 the difference to the owner of a potential stallion between winning and losing was several hundred thousand pounds. If he was late (which Lester still disputes), it was due to an unavoidable painful accident. The relevant Rule of Racing has been slightly altered. In 1952 Rule 168(lv) read:

> An objection to a horse on the ground of a cross, jostle or any act on the part of the jockey . . . must be made within five minutes after the winner has been weighed-in, unless, under special circumstances, the Stewards are satisfied that it could not have been made within that time.

How could they possibly have signalled 'All right', when the runner-up in the world's most important race was still missing? Were these not special circumstances?

Lester and I were both accused of having chips on our shoulders against authority. It wasn't that so much as frustration. So many owners, trainers and jockeys, who had reached the top of the tree in racing before the war, expected to carry on just the same as though nothing had happened. They, the officials and most of the members of the Jockey Club and the Turf Club could not or would not understand that the ten years which included the war had shattered the whole structure of society in these islands. As has been said on more than one

Above (left to right): Atty Persse, father, Uncle Rufus and
Geoffrey Brooke with the Limerick Foxhounds.

Below: Hurst Park, 1931.
Father driving home another winner!

Left: Myself aged three . . .
it seems I had problems even then!

Middle: Four years old.

Right: This pony, called Snowball, was a stallion.
He put me off riding from the age of five
after he had savaged me.

The 'All-Irish Kid' at thirteen.

Above: Now aged twenty, at Maddenstown.

Below: Riding out on the Curragh on one
of our horses at Maddenstown.

One of my very first winners—
Dorothy Paget's Plumage on the sands at Laytown.

Above: With my father in the ring at Leopardstown (1954).

Below: I'm trying hard to look sophisticated in 'the hat' at twenty-three!

Myself on Black Ice (left) beating Chiron in the
Daily Express Triumph Hurdle at Cheltenham (April, 1966).

occasion, when a major world crisis has been greeted by record prices at the sales, racing people only seem to read *The Sporting Life* and the back pages of the other papers. They only knew that they liked their little world as they knew it and resented any interference.

They tolerated successful teenagers, as long as they were ordinary apprentices, obedient to their masters, who touched their caps and generally 'knew their place'. This they were used to. This they understood. But when the interference came from thrusting, dedicated, independent sixteen-year-olds, who cared for nobody and nothing except their intense zeal to ride winners, talk about the generation gap! How could such men possibly understand the entirely new democratic thinking of the young Piggott and the same spirit which was trying to find expression in the priest-ridden mind of young Beasley.

This feeling, which I didn't recognise, was crystallised one evening, when Captain Charlie Rogers made one of his periodical big spit and polish inspections. My father had a large, highly efficient staff, including a Headman, Travelling Headman, Yardman, etc. During his inspection of the front yard, Rogers, very tall and, to my young mind, far too pompous and conceited, found a few oats in the bottom of the water trough, where the lads had been swilling out and filling their buckets. It was, of course, the Headman's job to have it cleaned out. But Rogers suddenly turned on Father in a rage and read him the riot act in front of all his lads. I snatched up a pitch-fork and would have run him through there and then, if two of the lads hadn't grabbed my arms and stopped me. From that day for many years to come I nursed a sense of injustice. It became a case of 'them and me' and my little brushes with authority later in life stem from that incident.

Driving back home after my first winner, Father said: 'Leopardstown seems to be a lucky course for us.' He recalled how he had ridden Golden Fleece, carrying 12 st 7 lb, to win one of Ireland's biggest steeplechases, the Leopardstown Chase in March. Two months later on the same horse with 9 st 7 lb he had won a sprint handicap at the Curragh. They were certainly a versatile pair—he and the horse.

But Father was already a sick man. He had the most dreadful indigestion and could not eat anything. He lived on soup. He was to live for another six years. It was too late when the doctor, who had been treating him for indigestion, discovered that all the time the trouble was caused by a growth in his food passage, which got larger and spread until it killed him. It was obviously this, coupled with near religious mania and natural introspective reticence, that made him constantly appear sad.

The Turf Club Senior Steward, Major Victor McCalmont, son of Mr Jinks' owner, said the other day: 'My father used to tell me that Harry Beasley was exactly the opposite of his father, the grand old man, Harry Beasley senior. He always looked miserable.' Looking back, I have to agree. Of course it would certainly have helped later, if I could have acquired his horror of drink. But he even went about that the wrong way, so that until his death I wore a 'Pioneer Pin' at all times, parading my teetotalism smugly wherever I went. I abhor this form of exhibitionism. I'd have learnt more if he had read out the parable of the Pharisee and the publican every week.

So here I was, the 'All-Irish Kid', who'd ridden his first winner and was on his way. I practised riding racing finishes on those poor ponies with renewed vigour the following afternoon.

One day soon afterwards I nearly wrecked that promising career. Somehow my brother and three other boys persuaded me to leave the ponies for a little while to play cricket with them on the Curragh. It was a sort of rag game. I was fielding too close to the bat on the leg side, day-dreaming as usual about racing, when my brother took an almighty swing at the ball. I never saw it coming out of the sun as it hit me smack in the face, splitting it wide open and knocking me out.

I woke to see a great big man like a butcher with a huge red face and hands wearing an apron covered in blood. 'You're a lucky young man,' said Ireland's most brilliant surgeon, Boucher Hayes. 'I've put sixty stitches in your face. Not only was your spine nearly severed by the force of the blow, but six months ago you'd have died for certain. We hadn't the antibiotics to stop the infection. So it wouldn't have healed and you'd be dead.'

I'm told that I showed no gratitude to my saviour. 'I have lived,' I said in a weak, but holy voice, 'to win the Grand National.' Rather like Joan of Arc and her voices!

The Irish turf authorities in their wisdom do not stage so many bumper races in mid-summer, when the hard ground could so easily damage the legs of big, young potential jumpers—those legs upon which so much will depend in the future. So during June I had only two rides, finishing fourth and fifth on a horse called My Deal at Limerick Junction and Mullingar—a quaint place to be when the attention of nearly all the racing world was centred on Royal Ascot, where our old family friend, Atty Persse, was winning the Royal Hunt Cup with Dermot McCalmont's Queen of Sheba. But, as far as I was concerned, Mullingar was a more important meeting than Ascot that day.

Nor did I even know that the famous Newmarket July meeting was taking place on July 16, when I went to Killarney to ride Touareg again. But, incidentally, I was to learn later that the betting market is much stronger at this little jumping fixture in beautiful Co. Kerry than it is at the 'Headquarters of Racing'. They don't turn a hair if a backer has a £5,000 bet at Killarney. But just watch the reaction if he tries to wager that sort of sum with the so-called big boys at Newmarket in July.

Funnily enough, although I rode for many betting owners and trainers in my career, I have never felt the urge to back a horse. Fortunately this is one of the few vices with which I have never been inflicted.

Anyway Mr H. Beasley was as pure as the driven snow that day when, as the outsider of four, he drove his horse home on the firm going to win by half a length. The other three runners had all won their previous races. After another ride ten days later at Down Royal, I had to wait until August 18 until I was in action again. It was unbearable. I spent the time riding, running and skipping. But it was worth waiting for. I had two rides and won on both. A double in my first year. Both horses, Touareg and Plumage, belonged to Dorothy Paget. I was having my first experience of Laytown, the racecourse on the beach, or the strand, as we call it in Ireland. I can't imagine any other country staging licensed racing with good jockeys and fair horses in these conditions. You have to wait for the tide, with the result that the first race may be run at any time. For the longer races you have to gallop six furlongs back down the course, turn round a pole and race back again. Some horses don't get round and disappear in the direction of Drogheda. Quite a number have ended up in the sea!

Both races were desperately close run affairs. Touareg won the $1\frac{1}{4}$-mile Gormanstown Plate by a neck and I rode an even stronger finish in the five-furlong Neptune Plate to get Plumage home by a short head. Unhappily owing to a newspaper strike in Ireland at the time I didn't receive the publicity to which I felt I was entitled. It was very frustrating. My contemporaries had seven years start. I needed every possible aid to catch them up and beat them.

After this, my fourth win in the Paget blue and yellow silks, my father and Charlie Rogers suggested that perhaps the lucky owner might like to give her jockey a present. 'Nonsense,' said Miss P. '*He* should be paying *me* for the privilege of riding my horses!'

Before that first year ended I had won two more races at Baldoyle and Naas. You will notice how my father was giving me experience of all the different tracks. Both horses, Royal Lodge and Royal Victory, were backed down to favouritism. They were trusting me with their money now. I had arrived.

Dorothy Paget was quite wrong, of course, about the presents. I was also being trusted with her valuable young horses, which I could so easily have ruined. If I had not given nice educational races to horses like Royal Lodge and Nickleby, they would have had no future in England. And I could have saved her a lot of money if she had asked me, by telling her that others, like Packard and Fair West, were thieves, soft and not worth persevering with. The attitude that the jockey is lucky to be riding for the trainer and his owner is one of the curses of Irish racing, which was to have disastrous effects on my life. For the moment, however, it was a great thing for a boy to be riding for 'D.P.' On one of hers in a bumper you started with psychological advantage of at least 5 lb.

The advantage of bumpers is that they go on all through the winter. But this was tantalising for me because I wanted to take part in the hurdle races and steeplechases, which formed the main part of the programme at these meetings. Now my spare afternoons were spent riding the hacks over hurdles. I don't think they had ever dreamt that they could jump so fast. Also from the beginning of November I went hunting whenever I had the chance.

I had realised for some time that Britain's world superiority at steeplechasing owes much to a firm grounding in the hunting-field, whence grew the point-to-points, which were the origin of the great sport itself. All the leading Irish jump jockeys from my grandfather and his brothers down to Bryan Marshall, the Molony brothers and Pat Taaffe had been keen hunting men. Of course I had missed out on this, but now I was determined to make up the lost ground as fast as possible in every department. Happily my dedication was such that I succeeded.

Those who have hunted from early childhood are lucky indeed. They are always able to explain mishaps, learning to blame themselves rather than their ponies. Bryan Marshall, for example, knew the reason for his falls from the beginning.

'However badly hurt I was,' he says, 'I would be saying to myself: "Why the hell didn't you make him lengthen his stride into that one?" or "You damn fool! You should have hooked him up and made him put in a short one." I knew how

69

it had happened and how to prevent it from happening again. So I wasn't worried. Riding over fences presented no more terrors than it had ever done when I was hunting in Ireland at six years old.'

Falls are horribly different, however, for the young man without hunting experience, who has served his apprenticeship on the Flat, and is sailing happily along when suddenly he finds himself crashing to the ground. As he lies there, bruised or broken shaking his fuddled head, life seems frighteningly unfair. He can find no cause for this shocking pain. God has struck him down. He knows no remedy for a terror which he cannot explain and he loses his nerve.

That's why so few recruits from the Flat ever rise to the top of the jumping game and why those, like Fred Winter in particular, who do so, exhibit a standard of physical bravery and moral courage that is seldom found in any other walk of life.

My initiation came just in time and this, coupled with the amazing expert tuition that I was shortly to receive, put me right among the fortunate few, where I was convinced that I belonged.

There has always been a competitive spirit in the Irish hunting field, which is very useful for the budding jump jockey. Most keen followers carry racing whips instead of heavy hunting whips (crop and thong) and are out to 'win the hunt'. This attitude is frowned on in England, particularly in the provincial packs outside the Mecca of Leicestershire. The English are apt to pretend that they go foxhunting to study houndwork, whereas, in fact, many go just to enjoy themselves (and why not?) and others just to be seen.

Later in life when I lost my halo, I was to chuckle at the apocryphal Leicestershire story attributed, as far as I can remember, to Chatty Hilton-Green, one of the great amateur huntsmen. One day he was becoming increasingly fed up with a bombastic, loud-mouthed businessman, who, half out of control, was constantly galloping over hounds, defying orders to keep back. And when at a check this fellow's horse kicked one of the best hounds and the poor bitch went whimpering away, Chatty finally blew his top.

'Can't you bloody well control your horse?' demanded the Master. 'Keep back off my hounds and behave yourself!' Purple-faced the offender expostulated: 'Don't you dare to speak to me like that! I'm only out the same as you for fresh air and exercise.'

'In that case,' said Chatty between clenched teeth, 'you can clear off home, bugger yourself with the bellows and get both!'

Banks, peculiar to the West Country of England, are a formidable feature of Irish hunting. Like Tim Molony, I attribute a lot of my success to this early experience. They teach you a great deal more horsemanship and timing than fly fences. There's no give in a bank, so however fast you are galloping you must meet it right or you pay the penalty. And falls over banks are apt to be very messy affairs.

Tim, five times English champion jockey, says today: 'Bryan Marshall and I learnt an awful lot from the banks. I learnt style and finishing from the bumpers.' Until he turned professional, he had been Ireland's leading amateur rider, which I was now becoming. Point-to-points over banks were tough affairs and in those days we still had banks at Punchestown.

In the next two years I was really in amongst the winners and by the start of my second season I was already getting the best 'outside' rides—horses trained in stables other than our own. For example I rode for the famous old trainer, 'Ginger' Wellesley. I remember winning for him on Cliffordene and one day at Powerstown Park I rode a strong finish on Let's Face It to beat Phonsie O'Brien a neck. The green seven-year-old that Phonsie was riding was called Quare Times, trained by his brother Vincent. Two years later almost to the day he was to carry Pat Taaffe to a memorable victory in the Grand National, the third consecutive winner of the great Aintree chase trained by Vincent.

In the spring of the following year I had already won on a useful horse of Dorothy Paget's called Buckingham. But at Phoenix Park we were well and truly beaten by Lord Fingall's handsome bay five-year-old Roddy Owen, who was making his first public appearance. I knew he was a very good young horse, but I never dreamt that through him I was to realise my wildest dreams.

CHAPTER 5

Levitation

'Get back, Willie Robinson. Don't try and come on me inside!'
We were galloping hard into a fence at Baldoyle. I stole a
glance over my shoulder and saw that Willie was still coming
on. I shouted: 'Don't do it! I'm warning you! All right, you
silly bastard, you asked for it.' So I pulled across him in the
way I'd learnt and turned him and his horse upside down. He
broke his collar-bone. I had to leave the racecourse in a hurry
because his mother was looking for me to kill me with her
race-glasses. But Willie didn't mind. He'd done the same to
me before. I didn't mean to hurt him or cause him any damage,
but I believed these were the right tactics in Ireland at the
time. You wouldn't get any more rides for a trainer if you let
someone get up on your inside. It's always been the same in
jumping. Try coming up on the inside of Gerry Wilson, Fred
Rimell, Dave Dick or Bryan Marshall. And remember what
happened when Roddy Owen tried to come up on my grandfather's inside in the National.

But in Ireland in the fifties it was part of the scene. It was
the 'in' thing. If you didn't do somebody, then you would get
done. Another day at Naas, Frankie Carroll tried to come up

on my inside and, as I thought I had a good chance of winning, I came over and put him through the wing. Luckily he wasn't hurt, but I'd put him out of the way and I won. At that time I had this tremendous will to win. If something got in my way, I had to do something about it—within reason. While I was still an amateur and in my first years as a professional I was done on numerous occasions, but I accepted it as normal. One very famous jockey, who is still riding, was a devil for cutting you up. As in England, you could only object from the last fence or hurdle. I was very fond of the story of Frenchy Nicholson, the splendid English rider who retired soon after the war and is now the finest-ever tutor of young jockeys.

Coming into the last fence one day at the rear of the field, Frenchy spotted Dave Dick coming behind him. He let him up on his inside, then closed the gap and put him through the wing. When Dave picked himself up and made his way back to the changing-room, he found Frenchy sitting happily on a bench. 'What the hell did you do that for?' he demanded. The veteran looked up with his roguish smile. 'Oh,' he said. 'You've got to keep in practise!'

It was rough and tough, but I loved it. As with everything else connected with racing, I studied the technique ruthlessly, so that soon no one dared even to poke his nose up on my inside and very few tried to 'do' me for fear of reprisals. Although, of course, I never analysed it at the time, I suppose it was a wonderful way of releasing my many inhibitions.

Meanwhile back at the old homestead . . . (It's a wonder we ever knew our way home. We had fifteen moves in ten years and lived in three different houses on the Curragh.) '. . . as it was in the beginning, is now and ever shall be, world without end, Amen. In the name of the Father, the Son and the Holy Ghost, Amen. Make the sign of the cross properly, Bobby. And give that nice Rosary to your Mother to take care of. Wasn't that one blessed by His Holiness the Pope himself? You can carry the other one in your pocket. It doesn't matter if you lose that at the races or in the yard.'

The little daily family ceremony of the Rosary was over. We got up off our knees. My father spoke to me again in that weak, tired voice, now becoming petulant. 'Sit down. I want a word with you, my son. Sure you're doing very well in the bumpers—much better than I ever imagined you would. But leave it at that. You're still only seventeen and you're not ready to ride in that hunter chase at Wexford.'

'How did you hear about that, Father?'

'Never mind how I heard. Just you do as I say. You're not to ride. That's all there is to it.'

'I'm sorry, Father, I've got to do it. I must start jumping at once.' I got up and left the room rather than listen to any more argument.

It was the first time that I had ever flouted his orders. We were still treated as children, who should be seen and not heard. The illness was taking hold of him now. His general air of misery and pettiness was aggravated by heavy secret drinking to dull the pain, although I didn't know it at the time. His absence from work helped me. Because of my regular riding and steadily increasing flow of winners the lads looked upon me as his understudy so that I learnt man-management as well as a lot of horse-mastership, which was to stand me in good stead later on.

I rode that hunter-chaser Last Pact at Wexford. Of course the old man was quite right really. I ought to have waited a bit longer. I let the old horse get too close to a fence he turned over and buried me in the mud. We were both plastered from head to foot. I knew my father would say 'I told you so' when I got home but I didn't care. I'd made a start as a jumping jockey. Actually he said nothing, but just looked reproachful, sour and bitter inside when we went to Mass next morning.

And, of course, with the reputation that I'd built up in the bumpers, I was soon in demand over the obstacles and the winners started to come. One Saturday at Baldoyle, one of the biggest meetings, I rode a treble—three winners out of the six races in the afternoon's programme. The papers made a big thing of it and nominated me as 'Sports Star of the Week'. This was what I'd been waiting for. I was still only eighteen, but I decided to turn professional. I applied for a jockey's licence and was granted one on the Monday. My very first ride as a pro won. That was the start. I was in business. Now I started riding for anyone who asked me. It was tough and it was rough. Away from Leopardstown and the other racecourses near Dublin some of the country tracks—the 'gaff' meetings as they are called—were very tough indeed. There was one called Mulacurry, which has disappeared now, where you galloped through ploughed fields. If you didn't duck your head at one of the banks there, a branch of tree would take you off.

And I rode for some funny people too. A small country trainer had booked me to ride his mare at Mallow. As I weighed out and gave him my saddle, he confided: 'She's very well today. She'll win all right. A good thing!' I went into the parade ring and saw the mare right on her toes, jumping and kicking, in a muck sweat. She nearly got away with me on the way to the start. In the race she took charge and went like the clappers until she seemed to run out of steam at the second last. She took the obstacle by the roots and turned over, knocking me out.

As I came to in the ambulance room, I heard people talking and lay still with my eyes closed to listen. The trainer was in a terrible state. Poor little man was pleading with the doctor. 'Mr Beasley won't die, will he, doctor? Say he won't die. Jesus, I swear I'll never do it again.' I sat up and said: 'What did you do?' Alarm mixed with relief in his face as he admitted shamefacedly: "I meant to give her a Baby Power just to wake her up, but I ended up by giving her a whole bottle of the whiskey!'

After the races I always went straight off home. Then occasionally I would go off to the movies or perhaps to a dance at the Golf Club, where I'd sit miserably sipping my lemonade in the corner. Most of my friends, like normal teenagers, had great fun (or 'gas' as we call it in Ireland). They got boozed, went with birds and were generally wild. I thought they were sinful.

I was trying to behave old in order to help my image as a seasoned campaigner. When I was twenty, I bought a hat to wear at the races. I was trying to be sophisticated. I was trying to be a man, but I had the mind of an adolescent. I had no experience of life outside the little world of racing. I was becoming more and more immersed in the sport, increasingly cut off from all outside thought, a sort of dedicated racing hermit.

This is not to say that I had no rebel feelings. It was the era of rock and roll. I was crazy about that music. It aroused sensations that I didn't understand and could scarcely bear. I suppose there has always been a certain glamour about jockeys and by the time I was twenty, I was among the better ones. A gorgeous girl, a 'raver', took a fancy to me. She persuaded me to take her to a few dances and wanted to spend the afternoons with me when I wasn't racing. She was very daring. She wore jeans, which was a terrible thing in those days. She was a fast bird and I was mad for her. She wanted me and I wanted her. God, how I longed to make love to her. But I was terrified of sex. Even to think of what I wanted to do with her was such a sin that I put it out of my mind and made jumps. Every afternoon at home I spent making jumps and then riding the hacks over them. Still I couldn't get it right out of my system. I tried every way I knew.

Through the curtain into the small dark room. Kneel at the prie-dieu in front of the grille. Make the sign of the cross.

'Bless me, Father, for I have sinned. It's a week since my last confession. I've been selfish and uncharitable. I've used bad language and I've been late for Mass through my own fault.'

Pause. 'Yes, my son?' He's not going to make it any easier for me. He knows damn well what I'm going to say because I say it every week. And he knows how much it embarrasses me.

'Father, I've been having bad thoughts.'

'What sort of thoughts, my son?'

'About girls, Father. About love.'

'Any particular girl?'

'Yes, Father.'

'Well, Bobby, you'll just have to stop seeing her. That's all there is to it. I know the girl and she's not for you. Already there's a hint of scandal because you've been seen about with her. And scandal's another sin.

'Make no mistake. Your thoughts are wicked and sinful. This is not love, but unholy lust. Yes, lust, my son. Our Blessed Lord has graciously given us the sacrament of Holy Matrimony for the union of man and woman in order to produce children in His name. Anything else is the work of the devil. You must banish these evil thoughts or face eternal damnation. Is there anything more you wish to tell me?'

Parrot-wise I repeat the old formula. 'For these and all the other sins I cannot now remember I humbly ask forgiveness from God and penance and absolution from you, Father.'

The disembodied voice starts again. I know in my heart that this is all wrong, but I must listen to the familiar strictures, followed by the hearty, patronising ending, which, despite the savage penance, heralds the inevitability barely disguised begging for a tip after Mass.

'I will give you absolution, my son. But see that you mend your ways. I should have thought you had enough to think about with all these rides and lovely winners. Your body's healthy enough, God knows. Keep your mind the same. For your penance you will say the Blessed Rosary five times and make a proper act of contrition. *Benedicat ... In nomine Patris et Filii et Spiritui Sancti, Amen.* Go in peace, my child, and pray for me.'

I come out of the confessional, feeling that I've been in there an age, keeping people waiting, and that all eyes are on me, sensing my awful guilt. I keep my fingers clasped in front of me in the approved fashion and walk back with head bowed in humility to kneel in my pew.

The priest, now full of bonhomie, is waiting to greet us as we leave church after Mass. 'That was a great winner you rode at Leopardstown yesterday, Bobby. 8 to 1 too! Wouldn't Brookling just about win again in the Galway Plate?'

The eager, greedy, almost cringing look so soon after the vindictive hectoring in the confessional was usually too much for me. I suppose I ought to have rushed back to confession because I knew darned well that Brookling had no chance of beating Amber Point when they met again in a fortnight's time. Paddy Sleator's horse had been very unlucky and he needed the race. I had an opportunity of getting my own back in a small way. I didn't mention the two 'good things' I was due to ride in the meantime, and I replied: 'Yes, Father, Brookling should surely win the big one all right', not caring if he lost the whole collection on it.

The Galway meeting is run once a year at the end of July or the beginning of August. As it therefore clashes with England's ultra-fashionable Flate-race fixture at Goodwood, it receives little notice across the sea. Nevertheless it features some excellent events, notably the Galway Plate, a $2\frac{3}{4}$-mile steeplechase, which I was to win six times.

The year 1957 was important not just because it marked my coming of age—in so many ways I was still a child. After riding for five years I was mature in racing alone. I was firmly established as a star in the little firmament of Irish racing and, of course, although it is hard for a foreigner to understand, bloodstock has long been the major industry in our country.

I looked back on five years of solid dedication and undoubted achievement. I knew everybody in the game and I was riding for the best of them—men like Danny Morgan and Tom Dreaper. I accepted without question the Irish outlook on racing, which still persists in the last quarter of the twentieth century. It is relevant to explain what I mean.

However young they may be, leading jump jockeys in England are placed on a pedestal. As long as they continue to prove their ability in an exacting school and deliver the goods, they are regarded as stars, glamorous personalities, who are in short supply and receive the payment to which they are entitled. They are treated as friends and equals by the top owners and trainers and many of the lesser trainers are honoured to have them riding their horses. They can hold their heads high and walk tall in any company.

The exact opposite is the case in Ireland, where every member of the population reckons to know all about racing. As in other respects, the country, which was mechanised a comparatively short while ago, is still years behind the times. In many ways, of course, this constitutes much of Ireland's charm and is indeed one of the main lines in the publicity repertoire of the tourist trade. On the flat the jockeys are paid a pittance compared with their English counterparts. And even jumping jockeys are apt to be treated like glorified grooms. The clock stays firmly fixed at a time when they were lucky to be given rides at all and regarded as benefactors trainers, who, in turn, took advantage of the situation and paid the minimum that they could get away with. Although it is strictly against the rules, there are still jockeys riding for half the official fee. The trouble is that, if they stick out for more, there are plenty of others only too grateful to take their place. Grateful. That's what an Irish jockey is always supposed to feel towards his trainer. Grateful and in some way subservient. There are so many grand young lads riding their lives away for nothing who would really make good if they would only take the step and get a job in England.

In addition I had learnt and automatically adopted the jumping jockeys' morality, which has always applied equally in England and Ireland. It can be summed up briefly as loyalty to your owner and trainer. To your employers in other words—as long as they don't ask you to do anything definitely dishonest.

We understand our horses and therefore we appreciate the trainer's problems. Flat jockeys don't feel for their horses like jumping jockeys. They can get up on them, knock hell out of them and they're gone. Jumping jockeys live with them, work them, school them, race them, and share dangers with them, so that they become part of our lives. And, of course, our living depends on them. The jumping jockey has more horse-sense and should make a better trainer.

The top-class trainers, for whom I rode, studied their horses with me. It is so easy to spoil a jumper by giving him a hard race when he is not ready for it mentally, let alone physically. Take two extreme cases, Mandarin and Charlie Potheen, two of the best post-war chasers, both trained by the master, Fulke Walwyn. They had terrible falls, at Chepstow and Newbury respectively, which destroyed their confidence. Charlie may never again be the horse he was. Mandarin came back to win the Gold Cup and the French National after Fulke had sympathetically restored his confidence. Many jumpers are lazy and do little at home, so that it takes the excitement of a race-course to make them exert themselves thoroughly. Inevitably, such a horse will require one or two races to bring him to the peak of his fitness. So my orders were frequently those which Atty Persse had many times given my father: 'Get as close as you can, but don't give him a hard race.' This can lead to hard words from the 'riders on the stands', who are usually talking through their pockets, particularly when it happens in the middle of the season. For one reason or another, a good horse may require a rest and, when he returns to the racecourse, he is not fully wound up.

So I used to consider that the trainer was number one. I was working for him. And, even if he asked me to give a horse an easy race, I was still working for him. It was in the interests of the firm. This was the morality on which I had been brought up. I never deviated from it, except on those occasions when I found I was going better than the trainer had expected and rode the horse out with hands and heels to win unfancied. If the trainer didn't like that, it was just too bad. The jumping jockeys consider you are 'bent' if you stop a horse that is fancied by the trainer, who has told you to win.

4—SS * *

This I never did. The temptations were enormous as I will recount later. It's worth a lot of money to a bookmaker or a professional backer to know that a favourite is not trying, so that he can lay against it. That's the worst of the bookmaker system. It's all too easy for a jockey to succumb. I like the story of that fine Flat-race rider Tommy Bartlam, who retired in the fifties and trained for a short time until he found that he was pouring his hard-earned money down the drain. He had a few jumpers and one day at a winter meeting Tommy, who knew the Flat inside out, exclaimed, 'I do like this game. The jockeys cheat fair!' It's a good description. Most of the jump jockeys share the same way of thinking. Of course, there are a few . . . but then there are black sheep in every walk of life. My father's last words to me were: 'Don't stop them, Bobby. Whatever you do, keep straight. Promise me.' I did and I kept my promise. I was never 'bent'. Even at my very worst, I never sank low enough for that.

Thumbing through the scrap-books and looking back on those early years, I find that I had an almost narcissistic obsession with my own image. This is fairly normal among young sportsmen who are constantly in the public eye. Besides, what else had I to concentrate on other than this career to which I had dedicated my whole life? When that splendid natural girl had hinted that she would be happy to shed her jeans if I so desired, I had run away in panic to make jumps. So the only pin-up in my young life was Mr H. ('Bobbie') Beasley, who, after December 1955, became just Bobby Beasley, variously described as 'brilliant', 'dashing', 'polished', 'most stylish', 'superb', 'powerful' and so on. Already that curiously over-used and abused adjective 'great' was creeping in. Fortunately in my case there was a formidable family tradition to live up to. 'The call of the Beasley blood soon showed,' wrote *Sunday Express* columnist Peter Morrissy. 'Bobby was a natural.' So, dedicated lover that I was, his description of me as 'quiet and unassuming' was, I believe, correct.

I am certain, however, that the Press with their ever-ready superlatives, spoil and thereby ruin a great many promising immature youngsters, who, basking in flattery, become big-headed and begin to believe that they know better than their parents, trainers and the senior jockeys. The trouble, of course, lies in the fact that there are far too few genuine, knowledgeable critics among the racing journalists. The vast majority have no way of appreciating the finer points of horsemanship. To them success, however gained, represents brilliance; skill, potential stardom. As the victorious teenager dismounts in triumph, too many scribes fail to realise that the winner, a decent, well-trained, cleverly placed, nicely handicapped animal, would have won in any case and has managed it this time despite all the clumsy, unbalancing antics of the luggage on his back.

Then there are the photographs—hundreds of them. Flat, hurdles, fences: close, thrilling finishes, easy victories: triumphant presentations, crashing falls. I used to have them pinned all over the walls of my bedroom. And that's not as bad as it sounds. By studying photographs of yourself in action, you can learn a lot and can then rectify your mistakes. Those pictures played a big part in making me the famous stylist that I prided myself on being. That was one description I reckon I deserved.

CHAPTER 6

In the Beasley Tradition

'AMATEUR JOCKEY STAR BEASLEY HAS
TURNED PRO'
'BEASLEY CHANGE WILL OPEN AMATEUR RANKS'

I certainly liked the headlines when I 'turned' at the end of
1955 and when Brenair II won for me at Naas on my first day
as a pro.

One superbly inventive story, which I treasure, featured my
earnest, delicate twenty-year-old face frowning at the camera,
and was headed 'THE JAM OMELETTE JOCKEY'. It ran:

> H. Beasley, Ireland's leading amateur jockey, who turned
> professional this month was literally brought up on the
> turf. His father before him won two Irish Derbys and an
> English 2,000 Guineas, his uncle won the St Leger in
> 1937 and as far back as 1891 his grandfather, Harry, won
> the Grand National. Beasley is said to attribute his success
> to eating a jam omelette every day before racing.

Some young reporters shouldn't be allowed out!

Then there was a picture which made me very proud. It was headed 'IN THE BEASLEY TRADITION' and the caption read:

H. ('Bobby') Beasley, who had his first winner as a professional rider at Naas on Saturday, comes from a family with a long tradition of horsemanship. Our picture shows his uncle Willie on Francis Brown and his grandfather, the late H. H. Beasley, on Pride of Arras, returning to scale at Punchestown in 1921, when Francis Brown was first and Pride of Arras second. Grandfather Beasley won the race on Pride of Arras in 1923—when he was 71 years old.

So from that New Year meeting in 1956, I had a great start. But I soon found that it was far from easy riding as a professional. All those nice 'bumper' rides were now, of course, denied to me and, of course, nearly all the decent horses from our own stable were sent to England for their jumping careers. So, with a few exceptions, I had no firm base and had to take rides where I could. Moreover, as my father's life drew to its close, there was so much more for me to do in the stables, on the gallops and at home. Apart from anything else, we were constantly moving house.

This was one of Pat Taaffe's best years and his brother 'Tos' was also well in among the winners. Nevertheless, I believe I beat them whenever my horse was good enough.

I rode our own Royal Victory to win a chase on the opening day of the new jumping season, which was to include some highly significant landmarks in my career.

By the time we went to Mallow on September 12, I had been going well for several weeks and, when his regular jockey, Noel Sleator, was unable to ride Some Pact in a chase, Paddy Sleator, thought by many to be Ireland's best jumping trainer, offered me the ride. The horse was 6 to 4 favourite. I duly won by ten lengths and thought no more about it. Little did I dream that this moderate chaser (he didn't win again for two years) would influence my whole life.

A few days later at Leopardstown, I finished third in a hurdle race on Lord Fingall's magnificent seven-year-old Roddy Owen, who was later to put me right on the map. The winner of the contest was Mr What, destined to win the Grand National.

Now I started riding for Ireland's other great trainer, Tom Dreaper. I won the Cork Chase at Naas on his Caduceus and on October 25 at Gowran Park, the picturesque course in Co. Kilkenny, I scored a double with Dreaper's Dizzy in the Dicksboro' Chase and Roddy Owen in H.E. the President's Hurdle. What a wonderful grandiose name for an event that was worth just £202 to the winner!

When Lord Fingall and Danny Morgan decided that the time had arrived for Roddy Owen to race over fences, they asked me to come over and school him, help Danny teach him to jump the thick black birch-twig obstacles that are so different from hurdles. A good hurdler, like an American chaser, is always on his forehand. He just bends his legs to jump at top speed and is away like lightning, straight into top gear as he lands. A chaser, on the other hand, must learn to get back on his hocks and use the power of his hind legs and quarters to launch him up and over the much larger, stiffer obstacle. Timing is all-important. Get too close and you've had it. Stand off too far and you pay the penalty. This is why good schooling is so important, I still maintain that Roddy Owen was the best horse I ever rode. A beautifully made, all-quality bay with an intelligent head and a white star on his forehead, he had an incredibly long stride. He stands out in my mind more than any other horse. Yet the first time I went to school him, he fell four times with me. A long-striding horse is at a disadvantage when he starts jumping fences. If he is coming wrong into the fence, he must learn either to lengthen his stride or 'put in a short one'. The most awkward thing is when you have a horse coming into his fence absolutely right and then, for some reason best known to himself, instead of taking off, he 'puts down'—puts in an extra stride that takes him right into the obstacle which he hits with his chest. This can so easily happen to a long-striding novice. With experience and the help of his jockey, he learns to time and to adjust cleverly. A good jockey can make most horses take off where he wants and, above all, can judge his fence some way off. I reckon to be able to judge my approach ten strides from the obstacle. You can win a lot of races in this way. Stan Mellor was a wonderful judge. 'I, 2, 3, 4, 5, 6, 7, 8, 9, Hup!' You ask for a prodigious leap and get one, gaining that vital length which makes all the difference between victory and defeat.

Some horses are natural jumpers. At the first time of asking, they soar over their fences as though they'd been doing it all their lives. There's no point in schooling them. They know it all. Or they think they do. But beware! Like the young man who suffers from the same delusion, they don't. As long as all goes well, they are grand. They'll sail along in front, contemptuously jumping their struggling rivals into the ground. But when something goes wrong, as it inevitably will one day, it's a very different story. They slip, get a bump, are crossed or just simply find one too good for them. Then they don't know what to do. They have no experience to call on, no reserves. They are lost and thereafter they seldom regain that brash, overweaning confidence that made them so formidable. The mighty Mill House was like that. But look what happened to him when he had been collared by Arkle, the greatest chaser of all time. Far better the normal horse, who has to be taught to jump painstakingly, so that he is learning all the time. It may be a bit rough to begin with, but it pays untold dividends in the long run. Arkle was like that. In his first race at Cheltenham, he jumped so deliberately high over the top of every fence. In his last race on the same course, his third Gold Cup triumph, he hit the fence in front of the stands with his chest, but never looked like falling. Roddy Owen, too, was a long time learning. He fell with me four times that first morning on the Curragh. I thought I'd never get on to the same wavelength as this big, brave, long-striding awkward chap. But, after I'd won the Troytown Chase at Naas on him, they decided to let him take his chance at Cheltenham.

Every Irishman dreams of Cheltenham and particularly of the National Hunt Festival meeting in March. It's a sort of Mecca. They go over in their thousands and the place is thronged with them. You wouldn't know there were so many Catholic priests in Ireland. Whenever there's an Irish winner, it's greeted with the familiar whoops, screams and yells. Win or lose, the fun goes on all through the three days and nights of the meeting. The amount of booze that's drunk is nobody's business. It's one big glorious party.

I will always remember the first time I went over as an unknown green youngster, strictly teetotal of course. We stayed at the big hotel, the Queen's, and every evening I sat in the corner like a mouse watching wide-eyed all the great English jockeys whom I'd read about and admired on television. I couldn't believe it. They were way out. They just weren't in my scene. Some of them had been celebrating well and appeared far from sober. One of the most famous was crawling round the dining-room on his hands and knees looking for his false teeth, well pissed. I was horrified. I felt so self-righteous. Here was I, over from Holy Ireland, wearing my Pioneer Pin. I was protected. Christ, how could these terrible people behave like this! How could they possibly hope to ride a winner tomorrow? They were still hard at it when I went to bed, shocked and confused, before ten o'clock! I lay awake for a long time listening to the sounds of revelry.

To my utter amazement they turned up at the course the next day, hard, fit and full of fun, and proceeded to ride winners. Me, I fell at the first fence and broke a bone in my ankle. This other world—a world of hard men—was to haunt me for some years to come.

Back in Ireland, I kept quiet about my ankle. I had already

broken my collar-bone, which was a lot more painful, and, once I was on a horse, the leg didn't worry me too much. There was something far more important to attend to. I was to have my first ride in the Grand National.

Paddy Murphy is a wonderful man, a truly great friend, who has stuck to me through thick and thin. A tremendous character. He was a jockey in Ireland and the States, show-jumped at Madison Square Garden, and risked his neck hundreds of times as a film stunt man, doubling for the tough actors.

Now, although I was only twenty-one, he asked me to ride a mare he trained, Sandy Jane II, in the National. At 15 hands 1 inch, she must have been one of the smallest horses ever to race over those big Aintree fences. And they were really big. The course had not yet been changed.

Of course the papers had a ball. They headlined: 'GRAND NATIONAL FAMILY', 'ANOTHER BEASLEY TAKES UP THE TURF'S BIGGEST CHALLENGE TO MAN AND HORSE'. They wrote features about our family, about the little mare and me.

Typical was Peter Morrissy, who wrote a whole piece about us in the *Sunday Express*:

> Somewhere in the colourful maelstrom this year a lithe Irish jockey will be 4½ miles from fame. Twenty-one-year-old Harry ('Bobby') Beasley will be riding his first National. And spurring him on will be an unquenchable ambition to add his share to the family tradition that reaches back through Aintree history.

Under the heading 'Turf's Toughest men FACE THE BIG TEST', the *Sunday Dispatch*'s John Murdoch featured profiles of the Irish riders taking part with photographs of Pat and Tos Taaffe, Johnny Lehane and myself. 'Bobby Beasley has been a professional for less than a couple of years. He is regarded as the most stylish jockey in Ireland . . .'

Sandy Jane and her inseparable companion, a goat, were already in the Aintree racecourse stables, when I rode a chasing winner at Mallow and drove back 150 miles to Dublin to catch the night boat to Liverpool with Paddy Murphy. So I slept well, unlike many of the thirty-four other riders who would be lining up with me.

When we landed, we took a taxi straight out to the course, inspected the mare, who was in fine fettle, then walked round. From the ground the fences seemed huge—remember they had still not been sloped or bushed out invitingly as they are today—and I was struck by the sharp angle at which some of them were sited. I was to find that, far from noticing this when you are riding, you meet them all just right. There is a drop to each fence on the landing side, which is peculiar to Liverpool, and there are several awkward corners, especially after Becher's Brook and at the Canal Turn. Certainly the height and spread of the famous open ditch, the 'Chair', in front of the stands seem alarming from the ground, for the fence is taller than a man and 3 feet wide, the ditch in front is 6 feet wide, and the guard rail on the take-off side is 18 inches high.

Even on this first inspection, I realised that this is not by any means a cruel course, although it is no place for cowardly horses or bad jumpers. And there's plenty of room. The first five fences are so wide that twenty-five horses could jump them abreast without coming to any harm, whereas on some courses there is barely room for half a dozen.

'You've jumped bigger banks than these out hunting many a time,' said Paddy consolingly. But I didn't need any words of comfort. I was about to fulfil my life's ambition and, three quarters of a mile away from the stands, I felt nothing but the thrill of anticipation as I looked for the first time at the red flag with its white letter 'B' fluttering high over Becher's. As we walked back past Valentine's, recrossed the Melling Road and came back on to the racecourse proper, noting the extra long run-in after the last fence, which has drained the stamina dregs of many a good horse, Paddy discussed the race.

'She's too small to stand much of the buffeting that goes on in the early stages,' he said. 'But she jumps really well and stays for ever. So you'll be better missing your break and not joining in the helter-skelter for the first fence. Give her plenty of light when you're coming to it. Then just imagine you're having a good hunt and enjoy yourself. Time enough to start riding when you've a mile to go.'

We went back to the stables for another look at the mare, a pat for the goat and a final word with Ned Sherlock, who looked after them both. As always, Paddy's wit never flagged.

The time dragged by. I knew no one, but recognised many faces as the crowd started to arrive. I was amazed at the dirt and dinginess of the old stands where the world's greatest steeplechase was to be run. Eventually I was able to go into the changing-room.

The electric atmosphere was unlike anything I had ever imagined. Later I was to discover that there is always this air of suppressed excitement before the National. I wasn't in the least frightened, but, although I tried to appear nonchalant, I was frankly overawed to be sharing the same changing-room with my great heroes, Fred Winter, Dave Dick, Tim Brookshaw, Michael Scudamore and the others who had thrilled me on television. We had a few words with the Taaffe brothers and then Johnny and I huddled in a corner, watching and listening, taking it all in. Not that there was much listening, for most of the jockeys were unusually silent. For once even the smiles that greeted Dave Dick's wisecracks seemed to be forced.

We queued to weigh out, watched by the glass eye of a film or television camera. I thought of Father and Mother looking in at home. Then back to sit in silent rows on the benches in the changing-room. At last we were given the word to go out and I joined the owner, Mrs Lamb, and Paddy in the parade-ring.

Unlike most of the other trainers, Paddy was not at all strained or worried. 'Enjoy yourself, Bobby', he said as he gave me a leg-up. 'You haven't far to fall!'

In the parade, I was dwarfed by the other runners—Fred Winter on the massive chestnut Sundew, Mick Batchelor on Scotland's pride, Wyndburgh, Dave Dick and Tos Taaffe on the previous winners ESB and Royal Tan. As we passed in front of the stands, I saw from the bookmakers' boards that the first two favourites were Goosander and Much Obliged, both from the stable of the great Yorkshire trainer Neville Crump. Champion jockey Fred Winter, who had yet to win the National, was at 20 to 1. Sandy Jane was one of the outsiders at 40's.

I hadn't much time to think as the leaders were turning to canter back to the start and my mare was right on her toes. As soon as Ned loosed the lead-rein, she whipped round and put in a couple of lightning bucks. Luckily I knew her and was ready for them or my first National might have ended even more ignominiously than my first ride at Cheltenham.

Down at the start we walked round and round. We adjusted our girths and the starter called the roll. Then we moved in, all thirty-five of us, and we were off. The mare was so keen that, as the line moved forward, I had no chance of missing my break. We were so squeezed by the other horses that she was virtually carried along. Then the field went along so fast that she was run off her legs. She was jumping all right, but just couldn't go with them and, as they went away to Becher's, I could only see from my pony the jockeys' caps going up and down over the fences way in front of me. We were that far behind.

As I came to the eleventh fence, an open ditch, I found Pat and Johnny both out of the race having been baulked, but somehow little Sandy Jane managed to clear not only the obstacle, but also Much Obliged and Michael Scudamore, who had fallen there. By then I was seriously considering whether to pull her up. However, I kept going and by the Canal Turn second time round she suddenly recovered, got her second wind and began to run on, catching up those that remained in the race. It was too late. Our chance had gone. We passed more and more fallen horses, saw Derek Ancil go on Athenian at the second last and then David Gibson on China Clipper II at the last, and galloped on to finish tenth just behind ESB and Tim Brookshaw's mount Merry Throw. As I pulled up, I saw Fred Winter being escorted back by the traditional Aintree mounted policemen. The great champion's strength and skill had carried Sundew, despite all his clumsy mistakes to victory, and the cheers with which he was greeted were heartfelt.

As for me, although I pretended to be annoyed that I had not finished closer, I was the only Irish jockey to complete the course. I was delighted with my first National and eternally grateful to dear gallant Sandy Jane.

Before leaving the course we went to see her. The race had taken so much out of that wonderfully game little mare, that she lay down in her box for two whole days. And when we visited her, she was lying flat out with the goat licking her stomach, which was red raw. She had scratched herself every time she jumped over one of those twenty-eight big old Aintree fences.

I said the National isn't cruel. It certainly isn't today. No horse will race properly anywhere if he doesn't like it and most of the horses which run at Liverpool positively enjoy it. You'll see the first-fence fallers galloping and jumping round with zest to complete the course. But in those days, if you were as small and as brave as Sandy Jane, it couldn't have been much fun.

The National was still held on a Friday and as everyone was staying on for the Saturday races, the winning owner traditionally gave a party in the Adelphi Hotel on Friday night. It was usually quite a party! A jumping jockey's active life is a short one and a gay one. Most of them live on the principle of 'Eat, drink, enjoy the girls and be merry, for tomorrow may bring a very nasty fall'. So, when they let their hair down, they can be wild. A number of the trainers, too, have always been former jumping jockeys, some of whom may have fallen on their heads a few times too often. The Adelphi took a fair battering every year. Inevitably, crystal chandeliers, the huge glass fountain, and assorted items of furniture suffered, so that some of the bills presented and paid on Saturday's hangover morning were astronomical. The knowing ones remembered not to put their shoes outside the bedroom door for cleaning. The Adelphi has 284 rooms, many of them doubles. One year in the early hours of Saturday morning, about 400 pairs of shoes were collected and thrown out of a window, higgledy-piggledy on to the pavement of one of Liverpool's busiest streets. A great many people were very late getting to the races!

Since the National is now usually held on a Saturday, nearly everyone goes home at the end of the day, so the party, which is sometimes not given that night at all, is only a shadow of its former self. I'll bet that splendid hotel, built in the affluent days of the London Midland and Scottish Railway, would rather have those gay, hectic parties than be used as Harold Wilson's election headquarters.

Anyway there was no party for twenty-one-year-old Beasley that year. Paddy and I caught the boat back to Ireland that same night. It was packed with very drunken Irishmen, who had come over for the race, and were either drowning their sorrows or celebrating their winnings because many of them had backed the great Catholic hero Fred Winter.

The bar on that boat stays open all night. In recent years up to his premature death, Willy O'Grady took full advantage of it. One of the real characters of Irish racing, a former fine jump jockey turned trainer, Willy was always deservedly popular. He was one of those rare alcoholics that are never morose or angry, always the life and soul of every party, kissing all the girls who loved him, dancing on the tables—a proper little leprechaun of a man. Willy found that he could defeat the ridiculous English licensing laws throughout the meeting. By going backwards and forwards from Dublin to Liverpool, he could spend all his time drinking in company at an open bar—either in the Adelphi, at the races or on the boat.

I rode Roddy Owen into seventh place in the Irish Grand National at Fairyhouse. The handicapper had already appreciated Roddy's strength, so that he was second top weight and was giving more than two stone to the first and second, Killballyown and Brookling on both of whom I had won races. Nevertheless I'm thankful that I remained loyal to Lord Fingall's horse.

Despite my successes, I was still battling on as a freelance jockey. That wonderful man Gerald Balding, Britain's best ever polo-player, father of Toby and Ian, who have already won a National and a Derby respectively, asked my father if I could go over to England to ride as first jockey to his stable at Weyhill in Hampshire. Father refused on the grounds that I was too inexperienced and immature to leave Ireland. But he was by now growing weak and anyhow this argument didn't apply when I was offered the best job in my own country at the time. Way back in September, I had ridden that winner, Some Pact, for Paddy Sleator when his jockey, Noel Sleator, failed to turn up. Now Noel was on the point of retiring and Ireland's leading trainer offered me the job as his stable-jockey. I accepted gratefully, not knowing that I was taking the most momentous step in my life when I moved into my attic bedroom at Grange Con.

I was first jockey to Ireland's leading jumping stable. My retaining fee was my board and lodging.

CHAPTER 7

Svengali

Grange Con is a little old village all on its own in the wild Wicklow Hills. It has a church, two pubs, two shops and a few houses. It is rugged, very cold, and an ideal place for getting on with the job of training racehorses, free from interference or prying eyes, away from the commercialised racing centres. For the entire life of Grange Con is centred on the man in the big old house, the Guv'nor, who is probably the cleverest Irish jumping trainer of them all, Paddy Sleator.

Irish eyes set in a wrinkled Irish face surmounted by crinkly hair. Eyes that can be steely hard with cold rage, twinkling with charm and the mischievous dry wit for which their owner is famous or, for the greater part of the time pensively alert. A trim, slight figure, always neatly turned out, Sleator is a man who loves and understands horses and finds that love returned with interest. A difficult man to get to know well, he is liked and respected by both men and women.

Yes, Sleator is Grange Con. He has gallops in three different places. Just by the yard and the big house, where I lived (the stable-lads were lodged in digs around the village) is his own schooling ground. At the back, across the old railway line, which he has now bought, are the conventional hurdles, the short work gallops and the new one-mile cinder all-weather gallop. Two miles down the little high-banked road, where it's almost an event to see a car, and where horses, donkeys, carts and cattle are commonplace, are the main gallops. Seven furlongs round the plough and on the outside a good $1\frac{3}{4}$-mile gallop. In heavy, rough weather we switched to the stubble to avoid cutting up the well-tended turf.

When I arrived, the headman said to me: 'Now, listen, son. Don't you have any illusions about yourself. You're going to have to ride here to survive.' He was right about the riding, but wrong about my illusions. Of course, after only eighteen months as a professional, I was thrilled to get the job that all my rivals coveted. It was the start of a new era for me and I still remember the awakening feeling of excitement and challenge. I'd made the breakthrough at last. But, unlike some well-known jockeys, whose confident—even arrogant—personalities helped them to the top, I was never cocky or in the least satisfied with my own achievements. I had grown up with the attitude that you should be very grateful for what you've got and never expect to get any more.

It's so different from England, where ability is appreciated and often exaggeratedly rewarded: where a young man is almost forced to develop any latent star-quality and is apt to be treated as a star, even when he doesn't possess it: where a top jockey is a big man, a hero, an idolised pin-up. I was to find the change very difficult later. This attitude runs right through Irish life outside racing and is responsible for the fact that many first-class jockeys and other men never realise their potential, but remain bogged down in Ireland. 'Thank you very much for putting me on that winner. It was very good of you to give me the chance, Sir.' The bosses never want you to get too much praise, nor do they give you too much encouragement, because they want you to remain grateful in case they should lose their hold on you. This was the attitude of the headman at Grange Con and of most of the Irish trainers.

Paddy had it too. But with him it was subconscious. He was altogether different. It is very difficult indeed for a jockey to develop such an understanding with his trainer as we had. There was complete mutual confidence. In all the years I rode for him, we never had a row. It got to the stage where I was able to ask him: 'Is there anything you think I'm doing wrong and ought to change?'

When I first arrived straight from the Curragh where I had been riding flat gallops on two-year-olds and other high-class horses, I rode with far too short stirrup-leathers. I was the stable-jockey and inevitably the stable-lads imitated me, which was not good for them or for the horses.

Paddy bided his time. He waited for a big morning when a number of owners were visiting Grange Con, to watch the horses work. As we walked our horses round the Guv'nor and his guests, waiting for his orders, I was leading the string, riding with my knees right up, like Lester Piggott. With his famous long cigarette holder still in his mouth, Paddy said in his quiet, carrying voice: 'Jeesus, Bobby, will you let down those fuckin' leathers. When you're riding work, you look just like a dog fuckin' a thistle!' I let them down and so did the lads.

I was one of the family but I went to my attic bedroom early just as I had done before. I still had no social life and it was a lonely sort of existence. But it suited me. I had set out on a life of dedication and here I was with a dedicated trainer. I didn't groom any horses—'do my two', as it is called in racing. I was first jockey. But the headman was right. It was a tough place and a tough life, in which you had to ride to survive. I rode out four lots a day and we schooled the horses over the jumps four days a week. It was the greatest place in the world for a young lad to learn about riding and it was so lucky for me because, having started late and missed all the early pony club tuition, I was now, thanks to this intensive routine, able to catch up. Moreover, the work helped me to keep my weight down. When I first started riding, I was very heavy. Then, when I was seventeen, I had Asian 'flu and the weight fairly fell off. I had managed to keep it down and now, at Grange Con, I had no option. I've never been so fit in my life. This was to stand me in great stead later on. I feel sad for the young people of today, who grow up with no physical reserves for their middle and old age, because their bodies have never been really tuned up to peak fitness.

Not unnaturally, since he had been the great man's stable-jockey, my father was always quoting Atty Persse, who used to say: 'A jumping trainer is a man who teaches his horses to jump. If they fall, he is falling down on his job.' Paddy Sleator is a great jumping trainer, even by Atty's demanding standards. It was very rare to get a faller from Grange Con. This was wonderful for a jockey. When you had lived with Paddy and the horses, you went out for a race with such confidence. There was no worry about whether they would jump first time. We'd worked hard at it and it paid off. The main Sleator precept is that you only get out what you put in. He has infinite patience.

As soon as a young horse had been broken and backed, he would be lunged over a pole and then ridden over it. Next we would canter him round in small circles, nagging him over jumps made from six unyielding tar-barrels in a row with wings to keep him in and a pole on the ground in front of the obstacle to teach him to stand back. This taught respect.

Then we would let them stride on a bit over baby gorse fences with a solid bar running through, and again with a pole on the take-off side. When they were straight enough in condition to go racing, we would school them over the conventional hurdles. I was so fantastically fit, that Paddy always put me on the pullers. And some of them really could pull, even hack-cantering around. They were right up into their bridles. They were fit and so was their jockey—the recipe for mutual confidence and success.

If we had a bloody-minded horse who wouldn't jump, we would take him out and lunge him over the banks that bounded every field. After turning upside down a few times, he'd soon decide that it was better to jump the fences. Patience, patience! Giving every horse individual attention and time to mature, and studying their different characters—that was the secret.

There was no bloody-mindedness about one three-year-old that Paddy brought home that summer. This was a sturdy bonny bay with a whiteflash down his face by Roi d'Egypte out of Cissie Gray, a mare who had changed hands at different times for £8, £10 and £35, the price paid by Tony Duncan, the breeder of this three-year-old. As the stallion's fee was only £7, Another Flash, as the youngster was called, could hardly be called an expensive horse.

The cheerful, indefatigable bloodstock agent, Jack Doyle, a former Irish Rugby Football international, bought Another Flash at Dublin's Ballsbridge Sales on behalf of the Kerry-born London impresario, John Byrne, for whom Paddy trained.

When they went to inspect the unbroken three-year-old in his field, they found he wasn't there. He was in the next one. But he soon came back when he learnt he had visitors. Just for fun he would spend his time trotting around and jumping over the banks from one field to another.

As soon as he was broken and cantering, we started to school him. This was a natural all right, but not like those scatty ones I referred to earlier. Flash had taught himself, genuinely loved jumping, and knew just how to put himself right. I did all his schooling. Nice and steady to start with. He was so different from those sticky recruits from the flat. Brilliant. He'd have jumped out of jail. But he was a real character from the start. I'd be cantering him round on the plough, when he'd see a bird or something that I couldn't see and suddenly, without any warning, he'd whip out, drop his shoulder and, with a little buck, deposit me on the ground as quick as lightning. But he wouldn't gallop away loose like most horses. Not Flash. I'd look up and there he'd be, standing beside me, laughing. He was just like a rubber ball and I loved him.

All the time that we were breaking and making the young entry we were preparing for the serious business of the new season, which starts earlier in Ireland than in England. For me it was like a dream come true. My first winner for the stable was Knight Errant, owned by the attractive American, Anne Biddle, who had settled just outside Naas in Co. Kildare. He was a hard horse to ride and it gave me great satisfaction when I won the Dundalk Hurdle on him on July 12. We followed up with a double at Killarney and then on the last day of the month, we went to Galway to run Knight Errant in one of Ireland's biggest and most competitive 'chases, the $2\frac{1}{2}$-mile Galway Plate, worth, even then, £1,160 to the winner.

Although my mount, a hunter-chaser of the previous season, had never before run in an open 'chase, he was backed down to favouritism at 4 to 1. It was a strange race on a lovely day in front of a record crowd at this historic Ballybrit course. There were fourteen starters, including Nickleby, one of those horses that I had ridden to win 'bumper' races when he was trained by my father for Dorothy Paget and which was now trained in England by Bryan Marshall. He was ridden by Michael Scudamore. As the starting-tape went up, it caught in Nickleby's mouth and we were all recalled because it was declared a false start.

When eventually we were despatched, I took the lead, but Knight Errant was jumping so stickily that he soon lost it. In fact, I had some very awkward moments as he made a mess of nearly every fence and we were soon some way behind the leaders. This was lucky, because five fences from home Southern Dago and Box On were involved in a collision, which brought about the falls of both of them, knocked down Pat Taaffe's mount, the innocent passer-by, Villain of Lyons, who was going well, and interfered with several other runners.

I was still pushing and struggling too far in the rear of the field to be involved. But suddenly Knight Errant seemed to warm to his task, took hold of his bit and started to jump like a stag. Two fences out, where Nickleby was leading from

Brookling, I had moved up into third place and knew that I had the beating of both of them! I jumped the last upsides with Nickleby, soon had his measure and had no difficulty in holding off the late challenge of New Hope to win by three lengths.

This race, well illustrated, was splashed all over the Irish papers. It was splendid for me and a wonderful start to my new job. It also set the seal on my partnership with Paddy Sleator, which was to last ten years. He said that, when he gave me the job, he thought I had a lot of potential but very little experience. Landing a big winner so early, confirmed his opinion and gave me a confidence that I had never had.

Paddy really felt for his horses. Even when he had backed one, he would rather see me beaten by a head without giving a horse a hard race, than give him a hiding to win. As I came in to unsaddle, he would say philosophically: 'Never mind, Bobby. There'll be another day.' And there was, usually very soon. Moreover he used to place his horses brilliantly, very seldom running them out of their class. He would normally start in the smallest race and gradually work up. For these reasons, his horses lasted longer than those of any other trainer, except possibly Fulke Walwyn, the greatest of them all.

When I had ridden a bad finish, he would never be angry. He would just say, 'Jesus, Bobby, you looked like an old woman whooshing ducks!'

'Whooshing' is a nice Irish word. Some years later, four or five of us fell in a novice chase over the big, black staring fences at Leicester, vividly described by Dave Dick as 'concrete shit-houses'. I was going to catch my horse, get up again and go on. But Johnny Lehane shouted at me from the ground: 'Don't be a bloody fool. Whoosh it away!'

As that wonderful first season went on and I rode more and more winners for the stable, my intense gratitude to Sleator increased. He was the most wonderful man I had ever known. I would happily have died for him. In my dedicated, teetotal, virginal way, I was happier that I had ever been before.

Sometimes on my way to or from a meeting, I would stop for a word with an old Wicklow farm-labourer. Once he said to me: 'You young chaps have it all too easy. You can take a girl in your soft, heated cars. When I was courting at your age, I had to work for it. I'd have to lift a heavy field gate off its hinges, put in on the ground with my coat over it and lay the lass on top of that!' I laughed. I didn't really know what he meant. But I was champion National Hunt jockey, wasn't I?

I was still on the crest of the wave when the New Year, 1958, came in, winning at meetings all over Ireland. Indeed at the big Leopardstown fixture on February 22, I so nearly made racing history by winning all five jumping races. As it was, I won three and was beaten a head and a neck in the other two. I never noticed the rain and the mud when I swept past the post on Roddy Owen in the big one, the coveted £1,000 Leopardstown Chase. Carrying top-weight of 12 st, he had outjumped and outstayed all his rivals to win like a champion by eight lengths from Mr What, who was receiving nearly 2 st from my horse and who was to win the Grand National five weeks later.

Michael O'Hehir wrote:

Bobby Beasley, who is in such wonderful form of late, had the distinction of partnering a horse named after a rider his grandfather beat in a Grand National in the late nineteenth century. His win was but one of three for this popular young rider who scored on the Paddy Sleator-trained pair Prepayment and Casamba and was second in the day's photo-finishes on Floor Show and More Power.

So it was a very different Beasley who travelled to Cheltenham's National Hunt Festival on March 11, and, starting at 5 to 2 favourite in a field of twenty-two, rode Clem Maguier's Springsilver to victory in the Birdlip Hurdle after a thrilling finish up the famous final hill with P.X. ridden by John Lawrence (now Lord Oaksey), a very good amateur.

I was even more excited after the race when Tom Dreaper told me that Pat Taaffe, who had fallen with Double Crest in the Broadway Novice Chase, was too badly concussed to ride again at the meeting, and booked me for his three runners the following day, Anson, Fortria and Sentina. 'You've won on the other two, but I'd just like you to get a feel of Anson. Would you mind coming out in the morning to ride him a bit of work?', asked the courteous old man.

Would I mind! I was up before anyone else in the Queen's on Wednesday morning. There had been a fairly hard ground frost. I was cantering Anson round the inside of the track, when suddenly he put his foot in a mole hole and fell, firing me about twenty yards. I landed on a frozen divot and discovered that I couldn't get up. The ambulance took me to Cheltenham hospital, where they discovered that I had broken three vertebrae and would therefore be unable to ride for some months. It was the first big disappointment of my young life. Anson couldn't run, but the other two both won easily, ridden by Tos Taaffe. I often wonder what might have happened had I won on all three Dreaper horses. Arkle was only a yearling then. I always got on well with old Tom. Perhaps ... Well, there's no harm in dreaming, is there?

Anyway, I had ended up in the next hospital bed to Pat Taaffe. Soon we were in such good form that the ward was a riot. A chap with a terrible duodenal ulcer suddenly found himself cured. He said: 'There was so much going on, so much fun, that I stopped worrying and the ulcer healed up.'

But things might not have turned out so cleverly for me. The physiotherapist had me sitting up in bed doing physical jerks. Fortunately, a friend heard about this at the races and had the sense to tell Boucher Hayes, the great Irish surgeon, who had treated me before. That huge, kind man was dumbfounded. 'Christ!' he said, 'they'll paralyse him for life if they continue with that sort of treatment. They must have diagnosed something wrong. We must get him back to Ireland at once.'

As luck was to have it, my mother was at Cheltenham. Between them they got an ambulance, which took us to Crewe, where we spent most of the night because the trains were full up. Finally we travelled to Liverpool in the guard's van with the fish and the milk. When we arrived at the docks, there was a fierce gale blowing and the boat was heaving up and down on its moorings. As they struggled to get my stretcher on board, there was a sickening lurch and one end of it dropped over the side. I so nearly had a watery end in the Mersey, but, thank God, they managed it. Although I longed to be riding those Sleator winners, I was never so glad to find myself in a Dublin hospital bed under Boucher's care. I lay on boards for more than two months and missed my chance of being champion jockey for the whole of Ireland (flat and jumping) in 1958. I still topped the jumping list, but finished fourth in the overall list behind Willie Robinson, who had most of my Sleator rides.

As soon as I was allowed up, I went into hard training by the seaside near Dublin and the moment Boucher finally discharged me, I was off back to Grange Con. The come-back was nice and spectacular, engineered, of course, by Sleator, who had Ann Biddle's ten-year-old Amber Point all ready for the valuable Au Tostal Hurdle at Naas on May 26. I was 6 to 4 favourite in a high-class field and was fit enough to last out a gruelling three miles and ride a strong finish to win. In the few racing days that remained until the end of the season, I rode four more winners.

Then, like a conjuror producing a rabbit from a top hat, Paddy announced that we were going to France to run ten-year-old Straitjacket in the French Champion Hurdle, the Grande Course de Haies run at famous Auteuil in Paris' Bois de Boulogne. That was not all. First, we were going to have a look at the South of France.

Apart from my visits to Liverpool and Cheltenham, I had never been out of Ireland since the days of my infancy in England I hadn't learnt much since that time. I had certainly never seen a naked woman. I didn't even know what one looked like. After all I had no sisters and only holy pictures to look at. Moreover, even if I had wanted to, I would have been unable to find a magaine or book with any reference to sex. The customs at ports and airports were instructed to search for and confiscate such publications. Control was very strict. Even the *News of the World* was not allowed.

The French Champion Hurdle, like the French National and the Grand Prix de Paris, is staged in the middle of June, when Paris is hot and steaming. But Paddy thought that we needed a bit of a break. So we left early and flew straight to Nice accompanied by Ted Curtin, an old friend, who was helping Paddy. That night they took me to a night-club for the first time in my life. We sat right close up to the cabaret, the 'spectacle'. I didn't know which way to look. The nude girls came right up to our table and one of them stuck out a breast at me, so close that I could have touched it. I just sat there stupefied. The others, drinking champagne, were shaking with laughter. Ted said sternly: 'Pull your eyes back in your head, Bobby. You'll lose them!'

Paris was even worse. We went to a club called 'Le Sexy'. Again my eyes popped out on stalks. Now I found myself longing to sample the forbidden fruit. But forbidden it was. Even to think about it was a sin—a terrible sin.

Straitjacket ran well enough over the different type of hurdles, but as soon as the French turned on the tap as we entered that very long straight, we were left standing and finished in the ruck.

Back in Ireland life went on as usual. Father was very ill now, unable to eat anything solid, but making up for it with liquid refreshment of the stronger kind. I didn't mention my visits to the night-clubs, knowing how much it would upset him. He had still not yet told me the facts of life. The nearest that he ever got was to say to me: 'Your mother will get a bit peculiar once a month. Don't worry about it. It's quite natural.' That was all. Certainly, it's natural enough for a woman to have her periods, but I didn't even know about this until I got married.

My mind was confused after that trip to France. I duly confessed 'evil thoughts' to the priest, who gave me a blistering rocket and a heavy penance for my pains. I spent more time at home that summer. Mother's worry over Father was making her drink rather more than was good for her. She has never been able to live without dogs and has always been mad on poodles. She would go about the house with a puppy in the pocket of her dressing-gown. One day, when she was sick in bed and the doctor pulled back the bed clothes to examine her, two ferocious little dogs sprang out at him.

It was now, at the age of twenty-three, that I surreptitiously put away my Pioneer Pin and, having been emboldened by a glass or two of wine in France, decided that Ireland's champion jumping jockey could do himself no harm by having the occasional beer, provided, of course, that he remained fit and didn't put on any weight. The pressure to drink alcohol in Ireland has always been tremendous. However dreary most of our small towns may be, they invariably seem to have more than their share of pubs and this is where the men foregather. And, wherever there's a bar, be it in a pub or hotel, at sales, races or shows, you're constantly pressured into having a drink. 'Come on now. You're not a man if you won't have a jar!' or, as the booze starts to take effect, 'So you won't drink with me! Are you after insulting me?'

Once again we were all ready for an early start at Grange Con. By the end of July, I had already ridden nine winners, including doubles at Bellewstown and Galway. Another Flash was progressing splendidly and we knew that he was something special, but, typically, Paddy did not rush, giving the young horse all the time he needed. He was not prepared to ask him to race until he was absolutely ready for it.

I was riding so much for Paddy, that my old friends, Lord Fingall and his trainer, Danny Morgan, felt obliged to look for another jockey for Roddy Owen, who was being aimed for the classic of steeplechasing, the Cheltenham Gold Cup at the National Hunt Festival in March. It is called the classic or the Blue Riband, because, unlike the Gold Cup whose candidates aged six years and over carry the same weight (12 st), the Grand National is a handicap in which the best horses have often been beaten by their heavy weights compared with their lower-rated rivals. They engaged Bunny Cox, the top-class amateur, who was as good as most of the best professionals. I rode our old horse Copp into third place behind Roddy Owen when he won a little race at Gowran Park, the lovely undulating course in Kilkenny.

However, the combination did not win again, although they did manage to finish second to Lochroe in the King George VI Chase at Kempton on Boxing Day. Roddy was installed favourite to win a second Leopardstown Chase on February 21, but they could finish only seventh. I fell on Paddy Sleator's Amber Point, but I had noticed that Bunny was not getting on too well with my old friend, who was, as I have said, far from an easy ride.

Fate had played into my hands. Amber Point was eleven years old and that fall convinced Paddy that it would be asking too much of the old horse to take on the best chasers in the world at Cheltenham. After discussions with his owner, Ann Biddle, he took Amber Point out of the Gold Cup and, on the same day, Bunny Cox asked Danny Morgan to be relieved of his engagement to ride Roddy Owen in the big race. Feeling after Leopardstown that he was not suiting the gelding, he offered to stand down if another jockey could be found. Danny referred it to Lord Fingall, who agreed with the suggestion of a change. A jockey was available, the man who knew Roddy better than any other—me. I accepted happily. I would now be riding in both the big events at the National Hunt Festival, because we were sending Havasnack over for the Champion Hurdle on the first day of the meeting.

It was still a tremendous thrill for me to line up with my English heroes like Fred Winter, Dave Dick and Tim Brookshaw. Havasnack started a rank outsider at 40 to 1 in the fourteen-horse field, but ran well to finish sixth behind the great Fred on Ryan Price's Fare Time.

On that day the going had been good. In the evening it started raining and did so to such effect that it was soft on the second day. By Thursday the ground was so muddy and heavy that the stewards ordered one of the fences at a place where it was badly waterlogged to be cut out. As I arrived at the course, I felt just a glimmer of hope. Real Irish going, I thought, remembering that whereas we race in almost any conditions—and not for nothing is Ireland often referred to as 'The Bog'—, the English are inclined to save their tracks by abandoning meetings when the turf is heavy and sloppy. Incidentally, I always think this is most unfair on the owners and trainers of mudlarks, whose high action makes them useless on good or firm ground. And I knew my mount so well. Of course he was a very difficult ride. He always had been and I didn't in the least blame Bunny Cox for failing to get on with him. I had really studied Roddy and had found that it was just a matter of controlling him.

Nevertheless, although we were joint second favourite with the previous year's winner, Kerstin, I gave myself very little chance as I rode in the parade in front of the sodden mackintoshed crowd, whose umbrellas and bowler hats dripped with rain. John Lawrence was on the favourite, Fulke Walwyn's Hennessy Gold Cup winner Taxidermist: Stan Hayhurst rode the good mare Kerstin, Fred Winter had the 1957 Gold Cup winner Linwell: Dave Dick on Hart Royal: Arthur Freeman on Lochroe, who had beaten Roddy at Kempton: and Bill Rees on the quietly fancied tall, lean Pas Seul. There were eleven runners.

Let Louis Gunning, the excellent Irish racing correspondent, who now writes for the *Daily Express*, describe one of the most momentous races of my life:

The romance and the glorious uncertainty of the racing

game were never better exemplified than in yesterday's Cheltenham Gold Cup. Sharing in the spotlight on the romance side were three Irishmen with colourful Cheltenham associations—Lord Fingall, the owner of a really gallant Champion in Roddy Owen: Danny Morgan, who trains the horse: and Bobby Beasley who rode him.

Exemplifying the uncertainty of the sport was the absence of Saffron Tartan, whose rumoured cough unfortunately proved only too real, and kept him out of the race. And to add a further little touch to the picture, watching the race from the stand was Mr Bunny Cox, who less than a fortnight ago sportingly cried off the Gold Cup ride on Roddy Owen because he thought that the horse did not get on too well with him.

Roddy Owen was certainly a different horse altogether yesterday. He looked better than at Leopardstown and jumped with more confidence.

And while there are those who will decry his victory as a lucky one, the fact still remains that he came up that punishing run from the last fence to the winning line in the heavy going with dash and heart, which stamped him a really worthy champion.

Bobby Beasley kept his family tradition in brilliant style in using intelligence, opportunism and strength to delightful effect all through the race.

More especially, however, he shone in the closing stages when after being the best part of four lengths behind Pas Seul and the game, tough Linwell coming to the last fence he kept on driving Roddy Owen with that never say die spirit.

Pas Seul came down at the last, whipped across riderless from the inside and stopped Linwell, subject of a magnificent ride from Fred Winter, in his run.

It will long be argued whether Pas Seul would have won if he stood up or whether Linwell was interfered with at the cost of the race.

In my mind there will always linger the recollection that Roddy Owen was really running on with wonderful gusto for Beasley once he recovered from a mistake at the second last fence.

And, if neither of the other two had met with their misfortunes, Roddy Owen would still have put both of them to the pin of their collars to beat him.

As is always the case in the chasing championship there can be no loitering and Flame Royal saw to that in spite of the heavy going.

His jumping was inclined to be wild, however, and when they came to pass the stands for the start of the final circuit the rest of the field had closed with him.

He paid the penalty for his wildness at the fence past the stands when he slewed away at right angles on landing. He was pulled up not long after.

A new pacemaker Hart Royal had taken over at the water jump and he kept up the pressure as Kerstin, Pas Seul, Lochroe, Linwell, and Roddy Owen moved in for the kill. Beasley didn't lose an inch of ground in his beautiful run on Roddy Owen, but he was up against the 'master' Winter at his best on Linwell. This old stager and former winner of the race was making up ground all the way down the back stretch.

Kerstin burst to the front to raise the hopes of her supporters four fences out, and led Pas Seul, Linwell, Lochroe, and Roddy Owen to the next. She tired, however, and Lochroe and Roddy Owen were being hard ridden as Pas Seul and Linwell rose to the last fence. Winter's mishap on Linwell brought one of these demon-riding responses from him, and Beasley after passing him on Roddy Owen had to contend with a furious effort from Linwell.

The latter closed to nearly a length with Roddy Owen half way up the run-in, but Roddy's pace and determination carried the day and regained 'chasing's most coveted trophy for Ireland, who last won it with Knock Hard in 1951.

Needless to say the welcome for the winner surpassed all the other ovations of the week.

With Saffron Tartan out of the race Roddy Owen became a loyalty bet for many of the Irish at the meeting.

His owner, Lord Fingall, a director of our National Stud and one of the most prominent figures in Irish racing, had a great record as an amateur rider over the course himself.

Danny Morgan, who picked the horse for Lord Fingall after seeing him, at his breeder, Mr Andy Nolan's place, near Kilcullen, was in his day also a rider, one of the greatest of them all around Cheltenham.

Roddy and I came in to unsaddle covered in mud from head to hoof amid tremendous Irish cheers. My owner and trainer praised me and thanked me. I was so grateful to them and, in particular, to the magnificent big bay horse, named after my grandfather's Corinthian rival. At the time, I didn't realise the full extent of my gratitude. Only later was I to discover that he had put me right on the map, as a leading international rider. I returned to Ireland a national hero with offers of rides from all over the place.

The next day, when I arrived back in the yard at Grange Con, I was greeted by the old headman. He said: 'Now you've used up all your luck, son. So don't expect any more. Just so as you don't have any illusions about anything, you can spend this afternoon riding so-and-so over the banks. Just to bring you down to earth, in case you've got any big ideas!'

I was unlikely to get any big ideas about myself. But six days after the Gold Cup, I certainly got ideas about a horse when Paddy at last introduced Another Flash to racing. Starting at 9 to 4 on, he won a little hurdle race very comfortably at Mullingar. What a feel he gave me. He then proceeded to win his other three races that season. This was undoubtedly the best hurdler I had ever ridden.

It was sometimes very difficult when riding a good horse for Paddy not to win by too big a distance. He was fanatical about this quite rightly because he didn't want to expose the strength of the horse to the handicapper, who would give him more weight next time. After all, in jumping races, 1 lb is the equivalent of at least one length.

After several rockets for winning too far, I timed it nicely one day and, although I could have won by several lengths, I got home by a head. As I came in expecting praise, I was met with a scowl and the angle of the cigarette-holder showed annoyance. I was dismayed. 'What have I done now?' I asked. 'That was all right, wasn't it? I only won a head.'

'All right be buggered!' said Paddy. 'Jesus, Bobby, I thought I'd taught you better than that; the bloody horse had his ears pricked!'

I was proud that Father had lived long enough to watch on television his son win the Gold Cup. But now he was dying. With Paddy's agreement, I moved out of Grange Con and rented a big old place at Baltyboys just outside Blessington, so that I could look after the old man in his last months. I longed for a home of my own and a wife to share it. I was becoming positively broody.

In the early summer, I rode a winner at Naas. Nothing unusual about that, except for the strange coincidence that, although the horse was not one of Paddy's, the race was called the Grange Con Hurdle. And I saw a dark, extremely attractive girl, who was clearly no stranger to a racecourse. I asked several jockeys about her, and eventually discovered that her name was Shirley, and that she was the daughter of the outstanding Yorkshire jumping jockey, Arthur Thompson, who had won two Grand Nationals for Neville Crump on Sheila's Cottage and Teal in 1948 and 1952. This was my dream girl. Gorgeous, full of fun and brought up in the sport to which I was dedicated. Three years younger than myself and un-married. I determined to rectify that situation. I couldn't wait to meet her.

When I saw her again at Bellewstown a few days later, I persuaded one of the older jockeys, who had ridden against her father, to introduce me to her. This was my chance and I seized it with both hands. Overcoming my shyness, I asked her out and started courting—with no hang-ups, but in a desperate hurry. When I asked her to marry me, she said: 'You're not ready for marriage. You're not mature enough.' But she accepted me eventually. She had been brought up as a normal English Catholic. She was far more mature than I was and had no hang-ups about anything. One day, much later, a psychiatrist told her: 'You are disgustingly normal!'

Shirley agreed to a short engagement, but that winter Father died, freed from his agony at last, and we had to postpone the wedding.

By now I was so confident of Another Flash's brilliance that I was able to say: 'We'll wait until Flash wins the Champion Hurdle.'

CHAPTER 8

Consummation

After Father died, I moved back to digs at Grange Con. Mother returned to England, where her sister, Valerie Hobson (Profumo), was a great comfort, although she had enough troubles of her own.

Shirley came to the races with me whenever she could. It was normal in Ireland not to get married too soon after a parent's death, so our engagement lasted about a year and we went around together, having a pretty good time within the limits of my knowledge and experience. As champion jockey with a sweet, attractive fiancée, whose father was a famous man in racing, I felt good. I'd set out with the idea that, if things went right, I wanted some stability, a home as a base to work from, and a wife. I was totally ignorant about the deeper emotional side of a relationship and just had vague ideas about normal feelings of attraction. Marriage seemed the right thing to do, but I never gave a thought to the long term, to whether we were compatible, or to how it would turn out.

Although she was so much more mature and broadminded, Shirley was as fond of me as I was of her, and convinced I would grow up quickly after our marriage. So pretty and vivacious, so full of bounce and sex appeal, with her soft, brown hair, fresh face and lovely figure, she had no means of guessing at the narrow, inhibited hypocrisy of the Irish life which had nurtured her future husband.

She had a few glimpses of it, though. One evening at a Dublin hotel we met two Irish businessmen slightly the worse for drink. They confided in us that one of them had eight children and the other ten. They were looking for French letters (unobtainable, like other contraceptives, in Irish shops) to go off with a couple of whores. I was very shocked that they should mention such things in front of Shirley, but she was unabashed, and calmly asked one of them: 'Why don't you go home and chance using them with your wife to give her a bit of rest?' The man was horrified at the suggestion. 'Christ'! he said, 'that would be a terrible sin!'

Another reason for postponing the wedding was shortage of money. Even the champion jockey in Ireland got no more than his riding fees and 10 per cent of winning prize-money. None of those nice, generous presents that they received in England. No little fat brown envelopes full of 'readies' slipped surreptitiously into your hand, and, should you object, well, there was always somebody only too anxious to take your place. So, while I was spending my meagre earnings on living, travelling and courting—nothing more than chaste kissing, mind, even after the best evening out—I was waiting for my percentage of Flash's Cheltenham prize to get some furniture and put a down-payment on a small house. Just like the Doris Day movies which had formed the concept of marriage in my tiny, romantic mind.

If the ground was good at Cheltenham, Another Flash was a certainty in the Champion. There were no problems. He was a first-class, honest, straightforward horse. But he was unlikely to stay two miles in top company on soft or heavy going. So I watched the weather forecasts and prayed. My prayers were answered. The rain stopped and the ground dried out just in time.

Then the money started to pour into the ante-post offices with a vengeance. Flash had been backed steadily since the betting market on the race had opened. I look back on headlines—'GREAT DISPLAY BY ANOTHER FLASH', 'ANOTHER FLASH SHONE', 'ANOTHER FLASH—ODDS COME TUMBLING DOWN'. And so on. He had been backed right down from 100 to 6 to 3 to 1 and the bookmakers would lose substantially if he won.

Not only was I hopelessly green, but I was also totally ignorant of the seamier side of racing. I had never thought of jockeys being wicked enough to stop favourites from winning to suit the bookmakers. Now, of course, I know that the presence of bookmakers in the British Isles is the cause of most crime on the Turf. If bookies or punters know that a well-backed public favourite will not win, that he is 'dead meat', they don't need to risk backing any other runner. They can make the equivalent of a good bank robbery by laying slightly over the odds against the favourite winning and taking all the money on him that they can rake in. This is the reason for doping and for bribing jockeys. I was to learn that the temptations for a rider to become 'bent' are enormous. He can set himself up for life with great ease and very little risk. How much happier is the lot of a jockey in most of the other civilised countries of the world, where there are no bookmakers and the only big earnings are for winning, not losing your races. For this reason, I agree wholeheartedly with Wimbledon Champion Arthur Ashe, that the controlling bodies should act now to stop bookmakers from insinuating themselves into the other sports. But twenty-five-year-old Beasley knew nothing of these matters.

I was horrified, therefore, when, shortly before Cheltenham, I received a telephone call from England. It was a stranger, who guaranteed me the sum of £6,000 if I would stop Another Flash in the Champion Hurdle, drop him out and prevent him winning. I would be paid £3,000 before the race and £3,000 after. It would be delivered to me so discreetly that no one would ever know about it. As soon as I could recover my breath, I told the man to get stuffed and slammed down the receiver. There was I sweating to make about £500 (enough to get married on) if I won the race! Which, starting favourite at 11 to 4, I did with considerable ease in very fast time. Flash and I had all the banner headlines next day. The *Daily Express* article by The Scout (the late, immensely popular Clive Graham) was headed: 'A BOBBY-DAZZLER'. But I didn't feel very dazzling because I had collected a most painful kick on the thigh when Dunnock fell with me five fences from home in the first race.

All the scribes were very complimentary, but I particularly liked Louis Gunning's piece under the headline 'BEASLEY COMES HOME WITH THE FURNITURE':

Trainer Paddy Sleator's estimate of his Champion Hurdle hope, Another Flash, an hour before yesterday's race was: 'The one fear I have for him is that he may be a bit immature for the job.'

But he added this prophetic note: 'If he DOES win today, I shall be surprised if he does not retain the hurdling championship for the next two or three years.' There was certainly no noticeable sign of immaturity about Mr John Byrne's gelding, whose brilliant jumping and delightful action on the lively going marked him out the best hurdler to come out of Ireland since the legendary Hatton's Grace.

Bobby Beasley, wincing visibly from the pain of a bruised thigh after Dunnock's fall in the Cotswold Chase, was perhaps lucky, in the circumstances, to have such a trouble-free ride to his first Champion Hurdle success.

One sensed, from his confident seat approaching the last hurdle, that he had the other Irish runner Albergo well and truly mastered. And although Another Flash, after his brilliant burst of speed on landing over the last, was slowing perceptibly in the last 100 yards, his judgment was correct as Albergo was not quickening.

'Not enough mud for us', was the terse comment of Albergo's rider Doug Page.

The occasion, apart from its all-Irish flavour, was of particular significance for Beasley.

As he put it: 'Another Flash was carrying a lot of overweight today—carpets, furniture . . . the lot!'

The reference was to Bobby's forthcoming marriage, on April 25th, to Miss Shirley Thompson, daughter of the former star steeplechase rider Arthur Thompson.

Shirley was there to see Bobby win, and then to wish a hearty good-luck to Frankie Carroll on his way to the paddock to take the ride on Monsieur Trois Etoiles in the Grand Annual Chase.

'But for Frankie, I might not have met Bobby,' she said. 'It was he who introduced us.'

The good-luck message was well timed. Carroll rode one of his finest-ever races to score the first Cheltenham success for trainer Jimmy Brogan.

Bobby Beasley was hopeful that massage of his injured thigh last night would leave him fit enough to ride the well-fancied Solfen in today's Broadway Novices' Chase.

But although Solfen's claims have been boosted by the Champion Hurdle result—he finished third to Albergo and Another Flash in their muddy Leopardstown encounter—I will oppose him by Kilrory.

He was wrong, I'm happy to say. Solfen won the three-mile Broadway Novices so easily that his trainer, Willie O'Grady, decided to run him again over the same distance in the gruelling Spa Hurdle on the following final day.

I believe that I would have completed the famous big race double by winning the Gold Cup on Roddy Owen if Kerstin had not fallen right in front of us at the last and, to quote Michael O'Helier, 'so impeded last year's winner, that Bobby

Beasley was almost shot out of the saddle. Indeed, it was one of the wonders of the meeting that he maintained his place.'

I lost a stirrup-iron and was very nearly gone, but somehow managed to pick my horse up again and finish fourth behind Bill Reeson's Pas Seul. This was really a good result, demonstrating the rough justice of racing, because, after all, if Pas Seul had not crashed at the last the year before, it could well have been Bob Turnell's horse who won and not Roddy Owen.

However, I still managed to win another race at that never-to-be-forgotten National Hunt Festival John Oaksey ('Marlborough') wrote in the *Daily Telegraph*:

So Pas Seul's moment came at last! Amid the glorious excitement of his Gold Cup triumph—and of Lochroe's heroism in defeat—the rest could not be other than anticlimax. But two more deeds were done this afternoon which on any normal day would stand out as shining examples of courage and toughness.

I mean, of course, the deeds of Solfen and Albergo, both of whom had already run at the meeting and given their all—the one in victory, the other in defeat.

Solfen had galloped three miles over fences yesterday, and despite the ease with which he won the Broadway Novices' Chase it seemed a lot to ask when he turned out again for the Spa Hurdle. And as Ferryman's Image led him up to the last jump, apparently fresh and full of running, it seemed that the task would prove too great.

Through Vital Space. Solfen was hanging left between the last two flights, and if the leader could have denied him the inside berth on the run-in the result might well have been different.

There is, however, a short vital unrailed space after the last at Cheltenham, and here Bobby Beasley seized his chance. Driving Solfen like a man inspired, he caught Ferryman's Image halfway up the hill and put up what to my mind was perhaps the finest piece of jockeyship seen at the meeting.

Dazed and happier than I had ever been, I made my way back to Grange Con to ride more winners and prepare for my wedding.

Earlier that season I had won the Becher Chase at Liverpool over the National fences on a mare called Headwave. She missed the National, but came back to win a chase for me at Naas, the second leg of a double, which included a victory in the big event of the day, the Naas Handicap Hurdle. The runner-up in this good hurdle-race was a beautifully made grey, who would have been at the top in the show ring and had already shown his versatility by winning over fences, called Nicolaus Silver. He won a small chase at Naas on Grand National day when Merryman II was winning at Aintree, and, later in the year, was bought by the famous Worcestershire trainer, Fred Rimell, for 2,600 guineas.

When I said that I went back to ride more winners and prepare for my wedding. I put it in that order advisedly. Racing was the only thing that really mattered—more important to me than the biggest step in my life. Because racing *was* my life. I was only worried about how marriage would fit in with my work, what people in racing thought about me, what Paddy Sleator thought.

And Paddy wasn't too pleased about it. He considered, and rightly, that I was too young and immature. He thought that my career was going smoothly and there was no need for me to get married. He implied that I would probably lose my dedication, if not my nerve. He showed his disapproval by not coming to the wedding, which finally took place on the day before Punchestown; and took it for granted that I would be riding for him as usual at the big meeting as though nothing had happened.

What a stupid, selfish young fool I was to allow myself to make a heaven of racing and a god of Paddy. Selfish and blind not to see how unfair it was to Shirley to be married in the middle of the racing season to a husband who thought of nothing else and was not even prepared to give her a honeymoon, in which they could have found out all the intimate things about each other. A husband who knew little about the facts of life and nothing about the emotional, sexual side of love and marriage. I suppose I understood naturally the basic rudiments of my part in the act of love. But in love, as in everything else, I was completely selfish. When I was finished, that was it. It was all over. I was certainly not deliberately cruel, but I was just as cruel as if I had done it on purpose, because I knew nothing about the mechanics. I had no idea of how a woman should react or what pleasure she should get out of it. Shirley was a heroine, but we had got off to the most difficult start possible.

Younger people, reading this now, particularly in countries outside Ireland, must find it incomprehensible, pathetic, as though it came out of the Ark. I can only say in my defence that this was Ireland sixteen years ago. An Ireland in which there was strict censorship of films and reading material, where we saw no advanced television and where the men particularly matured more slowly than any others in Europe, because of our suppressed, inhibited, religious upbringing. Things are improving a bit now, but there is still a long way to go. So many different, tragic things were to happen in the five years before I finally grew up.

We have still never had a holiday—no honeymoon.

After my clumsy experiments that first night, we went off to Punchestown to be met by Paddy who behaved as though nothing had happened, except that the cigarette-holder was at its most aggressive angle. Of the two winners I rode for him that afternoon, one was a horse that had never won before, a 'maiden'. As I was unsaddling, he said drily: 'Well, at least you've done something in the last twenty-four hours. You've ridden two maidens!'

I won Punchestown's traditional top event, the Conyngham

Cup, which my grandfather had won many times over those famous fences and big banks and, looking back through my press-cuttings, I find it typical of my attitude that, alongside a huge picture of President Eamon de Valera presenting the cup to the winning owner and myself, there is a tiny two paragraph cutting which reads:

> Two well-known racing families were united early in the week when Bobby Beasley married the daughter of A. P. Thompson at Ferns, Co. Wexford.
>
> The name Beasley is famous throughout the world of horses, while the bride's father won the Aintree Grand National twice on Teal and Sheila's Cottage. Beasley was in action at Punchestown and rode two winners.

Then I'd put in yet another picture of the same race depicting Beasley jumping the last fence in impeccable style. Such were my priorities!

We had a nice little bungalow at Naas and Shirley took over all the worries which were beginning to bedevil me, as life became more complex with success—hotel bookings, plane tickets, tax matters and the constant problem of booking my rides as trainers telephoned, and ensuring that they didn't clash. I had been getting in a proper muddle before, but now, with her quiet common-sense efficiency, she made it possible for me simply to get on with the job. I congratulated myself on finding the right wife, particularly when journalists asked her if she minded about the risks that her husband was taking every day.

'Watch him ride—why not?' she would say. 'I watched my father hundreds of times.'

We had some very good horses at Grange Con now, including Sparkling Flame, on whom I won my second Galway Plate, Rupununi and the brilliantly speedy Scottish Memories. Sparkling Flame had a remarkable history. He was only a small horse, standing about 15 hands 2 inches, with a hollow back and a ewe neck. You wouldn't have given tuppence for him on looks. But he had tremendous ability and a heart as big as himself. Versatile? He had started in hunter-chases, in which he had a bad accident and was said still to have a rib sticking into a lung. He won a 4½-mile chase at Punchestown, won the Galway Plate by twelve lengths and still had the speed to win a 1½-mile flat race at Leopardstown with 9 st. Only a little pony, but a truly remarkable animal.

And tough. We had some owners in the yard, who had a wonderfully tough breed of horse.

It was Sparkling Flame who really started my English career. There were too few opportunities for all our splendid horses in Ireland, and Paddy had become increasingly aware of the large number of condition races carrying decent prizes at everyday meetings in England. That is, races which are not handicaps but are governed by the official weight-for-age scale and so many pounds more or less, depending on the value of races that a horse has or has not won. As the prize-money in Ireland at the time was a lot lower than that in England, good Irish winners could get in with much lighter weights than inferior English animals.

His friend Clem Magnier had made a few successful sorties. Now Paddy determined to have a go himself.

He started with Sparkling Flame, who had already won three races that season, but got into the Nuneaton Hurdle at Birmingham with only 10 st 7 lb. Birmingham was the perfect place for a first venture. Jumping and flat, it was an ideal fair racecourse, which should have been preserved at all costs. There were no 'ifs' about that track. If the horse was good enough, it won. Unhappily it has now been sold for development and the motorway near 'Spaghetti Junction' runs high over the site.

Paddy and I flew in to Birmingham airport in time for me to walk around the track. Perfectly level, with well graduated turns and a hurdler or a 'chaser had ample time to see and weigh up the obstacles before he came to them.

The Nuneaton Hurdle, worth £340 to the winner, was just the big race on an ordinary Monday card. Clearly, the English knew little and cared less about Irish form. The twelve-lengths winner of one of Ireland's most important races, carrying only 10 st 7 lb, opened at even money and, backed by Paddy, started at 5 to 4 on. Stan Mellor, Fred Winter and Tim Brookshaw were among the jockeys riding in the race, but, from half a mile out, Stan on Tokoroa was the only one with me and Fred Rimell's horse was giving us 21 lb. I just let out a reef at the last and coasted smoothly away to win on a tight rein by five lengths. Inevitably Paddy said: 'You made a balls of it. You won too far.' But he was pleased with the experiment and a fortnight later we were on our way to Manchester, another good course that has gone now, to run Scottish Memories in another condition hurdle. We won 'cleverly' according to the form-book and once again my victim was Stan Mellor, one of the very best and nicest of English jockeys, affectionately known as 'Smeller' by his fellow-riders. On the way home, Paddy confided: 'We'll do this more often from now on. Much more often.'

In the meantime I was concentrating on achieving another ambition by becoming champion jockey of all Ireland. Like other countries, we have separate lists for flat and jumping and I had already, as I have said, been champion jumping jockey several times. But, perhaps because so many riders in Ireland perform under both codes, we have a consolidated list and the champion of the whole country is the jockey who finishes on top of the lot. My father had achieved it twice, but he, like some of my rivals, rode 'jumping and flat'. I had to do it on jumping alone and, as we came to the last day's racing of the whole year, I was still one in front of the former champion, that fine flat rider Liam Ward, and one behind another flat jockey, the quiet, sympathetic Australian Garnet Bongoure, who was retained by the biggest stables. I was determined to win and for once I disobeyed Paddy. I won on Rupununi all right. Now it was Royal Meath, having his first run after a long lay-off. This was it. Paddy, who might never have heard of the jockeys' championship, told me: 'Get as close as you can, but don't give him a hard race.' With half a mile to go I was third last in a field of fourteen and was almost resigned to defeat. But Royal Meath was one of those slightly temperamental chestnuts. For example, he was funny about the head and refused to have it clipped, so that he looked quaint with just a woolly face and ears. The quiet, easy tactics had suited him and he was clearly beginning to enjoy himself. So I picked him up and gave him a backhander. He flew. Right through the field he galloped and jumped as though inspired. As we came to the last, I knew we had them all beat, streaked past Francis Shortt as we jumped the hurdle, and ran on strongly to win by two lengths—with his ears pricked!

I'd made it. And just for good measure I completed a hat-trick with Festival Hall. Champion Irish jockey for 1960. 'Stylist of the year', they called me, and the other jockeys presented me with a lovely silver statuette of a horse, at a dinner organised by them in my honour.

We had left Scottish Memories temporarily in the care of Tim Molony, who had just started training at Melton Mowbray in Leicestershire. And, while I was busy at Leopardstown, that great Irish jockey, who had been English champion five times, saddled our good chestnut to win the Deepfields Chase at Wolverhampton. He was ridden on this occasion by David Nicholson, known as 'Duke', because he stands 6 feet tall and was educated at a leading English public-school. A fine horseman and a great competitor, as befits the son of that outstanding jockey, Frenchy Nicholson, who now produces the best young race-riders in the world, including England's flat champion, Pat Eddery, Tony Murray, Paul Cook, etc., in a never-ending stream. David, too, is now training horses and jockeys most successfully and is so conscientious and hardworking that, in the unlikely event of my ever being an owner, he would be high on my short list of trainers.

On January 5, Paddy took me over to ride Scottish Memories and Sparkling Flame in 'chases at Stratford-on-Avon, a charming little jumping course on the outskirts of the famous town, deserving of all its immense popularity. Both won with impressive ease and I believe that this double really brought me to the notice of the English professionals.

Indeed, two days later, when I rode old Knight Errant into second place in the big Tom Coulthwaite Chase at Haydock, another excellent racecourse situated midway between Liverpool and Manchester, I was invited by England's leading trainer, Fred Rimell, to ride a young horse called Oblivious for him over those good stiff fences, two of which have drops on the landing side like those at nearby Aintree.

It was the six-year-old's first race over fences and we finished close up fourth, to the evident delight of the trainer, of whom I stood in some awe.

Before the end of the month I was back in the Midlands again when Scottish Memories reappeared at Wolverhampton, an interesting racecourse with some sharp bends that have since been improved, and a short pull up under a high level railway bridge. The late Dr Michael Murray, a great character and a fine physician, who practised for thirty years at Bidford-on-Avon and was medical officer at several of the Midland racecourses, had been reared in the depths of Ireland, miles from any railway, and had two passions in life, racing and trains. He loved Wolverhampton, where he could indulge them both!

This time it was not so easy for Scottish Memories because the going was very heavy. Len Thomas wrote in *The Sporting Life*:

IRISH RIVAL FOR 'BLESSINGTON': Scottish Memories will throw down the gauntlet to the smart Blessington Esquire in the George Williamson Chase at Hurst Park in March.

This was announced by his owner, Mr Gerald Sanderson, after the seven-year-old had won the Pattingham Chase at Wolverhampton yesterday.

'Bobby' Beasley, champion Irish N.H. jockey, flew over to partner Scottish Memories who is unbeaten since being sent over by Paddy Sleator to run in a hurdle race at Manchester in December.

Now in Tim Molony's care, Scottish Memories was winning his eleventh race for his owner, who lives at Dunning, near Perth.

Tim told me afterwards that in all probability the gelding would now return to Sleator until coming over for the Hurst Park race. Beasley rode a supremely confident race on Scottish Memories, but the gelding made two appalling mistakes which would have put many jockeys on the floor. He made a hash of the fifth fence, dropping back from fourth position to last, and then, at the next but one, slipped on landing and shot Beasley almost out of the saddle. Not the least perturbed by the two very quick mistakes, Beasley gave Scottish Memories time to settle down and kept his mount on the outside in order to let him see the fences.

Making headway, after jumping the water, Scottish Memories made a brilliant leap at the fourth from home which took him into the lead, but he was immediately steadied.

Two fences out Scottish Memories went on again, and though Beasley had to draw his whip on the run-in he scored a trifle cleverly by three-quarters of a length from Ragd.

'A trifle cleverly?' Little did he know. I'd hit the front too soon and I nearly had heart failure. Ragd was ridden by one of my great heroes, Dave Dick. Already, contrary to all my upbringing, I felt a secret longing to be a friend of Dave's and to be like him, a real hard man, possessed of charm and wit,

On Havasnack (1959)
(Sport & General)

Above: Cheltenham, 1959; 34th year of the Cheltenham Gold Cup. Pas Seul, ridden by W. Rees, falls at the last fence after looking an easy winner when leading. I went on to win the race riding Roddy Owen. *(Sport & General)*

Below: Cheltenham, 1960. In the lead in the Champion Hurdle on Another Flash, jumping the last hurdle to win.

Above: Here I am on Nicolaus Silver being led in by his owner, Jeremy Vaughan, after winning the 1961 Grand National at Aintree. *(Sport & General)*
Below: The victorious Nicolaus Silver after the Grand National looking very beautiful. *(Rex Coleman)*

Requisite and I take a hurdle at Sandown (1961).
(Sport & General)

Above: 'Bobby, you Irish bastard!
You said we had no chance, but he's not even sweating!' Arthur Thomas does
not look best pleased as I unsaddled the winner at Nottingham.

Below: Riding Rupununi on Arthur Thomas's
'all-weather' gallops at Guy's Cliffe, Warwick.

Above: Riding Richard of Bordeaux at Cheltenham in the
Mackeson Gold Cup, 1963—'I was inspired that day.' *(Bernard Parkin)*

Below: And coming in triumphant after the race!

who took danger, wine and women in his stride. I had long admired from afar this wise-cracking man who had the looks of a film-star of the old school, standing 6 feet tall with the build of a champion middle-weight boxer, which is what he could so easily have been but for being born a trainer's son.

It had to be Dave, who achieved every jockey's ambition when he was riding back after being beaten in a tough, gruelling race on a hot favourite and was greeted by a loud-mouthed punter with raucous insults accusing him of pulling its head off. Others ride by, seething inwardly. Not Dave. He pulled up. 'Say that again', he said. When the punter inadvisedly complied, the jockey dismounted. 'Hold my horse', he asked a bystander. He then dealt with the objectionable man in no uncertain fashion, jumped on his horse and rode back to the weighing-room.

A life-long friend of Fred Winter, Dave had ridden with considerable success on the Flat before his height and weight forced him to turn to jumping. Although soon restricted to horses high in the handicap, he was exceptionally good by any standards. His long legs were a great asset; he still rode an extremely powerful, balanced finish; his timing was excellent and he was as contemptuously fearless as his looks suggested. I wonder how often he was described as 'swashbuckling'. It was remarkable how successfully he telescoped his long, strong body, so that he was usually more streamlined than any of his rivals. A fine Liverpool rider, he rode Wot No Sun into third place behind my father-in-law in the National of 1952, and, despite the impossible burden of 12 st 5 lb, rode his Gold Cup winner, Mont Tremblant, into second place at Aintree the following year. In 1956, he won the National on E.S.B. He drove fast cars as well as he rode. A worthy hero for any young jockey.

This was my sixth win from seven rides in England that season. The future looked bright indeed.

Another Flash finished fourth on his reappearance at Navan and was installed as a very hot favourite to repeat his victory in the Champion Hurdle. Paddy Sleator had only one Grand National entry, Clipador, but Fred Rimell had several and, as soon as he learnt of the scratching of Clipador, he engaged me to ride Nicolaus Silver, the grey Irish horse that he had bought for 2,600 guineas at Ballsbridge. I rode him first at Nottingham on January 31, when he finished close up third after making one bad mistake. He gave me a good feel and it was obvious that he could be improved. And at Leicester a fortnight later, although we finished only sixth, he was jumping those big, black fences with a precision that gave me confidence for negotiating Aintree. That was Tuesday.

On Saturday, despite top-weight of 12 st 7 lb, I expected to win the big hurdle on Flash as a preliminary for Cheltenham. But there was a lot of interference in the early stages of the race and my horse was badly struck into. He never really recovered and, although he battled on well to finish third, we found as I unsaddled that he was cut about the legs. This was only superficial, but when he was led out at Grange Con on Sunday morning, he was very lame on his off foreleg. The vet was summoned and discovered that a hard blow through the crepe bandage and felt padding had bruised the sesamoid ligament on the outside of his leg. That was the end of my Champion Hurdle hopes. He was retired for the season.

On Monday I flew to Birmingham, summoned by England's great trainer, Fulke Walwyn, and his Irish owner, Sir Tommy Ainsworth, to ride the grey four-year-old hurdler Anzio, who had been a good winner on the Flat in Ireland. We started an odds-on favourite in a field of twenty-four. He jumped beautifully, as I was to find all Walwyn horses do, and we won in a canter by ten lengths. I was booked to ride him again in the four-year-old championship, the Triumph Hurdle, at Hurst Park immediately after Cheltenham.

I took the opportunity to go down with Fred Rimell to his home at Kinnersley, in Worcestershire, to ride Nicolaus Silver again. I was immediately struck with the gay, happy atmosphere of the place, presided over by Fred, another of my 'hard men' heroes, who had been champion jumping jockey before and after the war, and by his dark, attractive, highly intelligent wife, Mercy, a very fine horsewoman, who did all the entries, etc., and now rode my National mount out at exercise.

I knew that Nicolaus was a hard puller and was not surprised to find Mrs Rimell riding him in a double bridle. She has beautiful hands, but nine-year-old jumpers, who have been ridden by all sorts of different lads and partnered in their races by an assortment of jockeys, have been 'jobbed' in the mouth so many times that good hands are often not the answer, as they are with a light-mouthed puller on the Flat. You need the sheer strength of a man. Having ridden Nicolaus, I was amazed how well Mrs Rimell did. But every now and again, she inevitably came up the gallops slightly out of control to the delight of the lads and of Fred, who would shout after her good-humouredly. Psychologically this was exactly what Nicolaus wanted and the Rimells knew it. Far from being bullied, he felt that he was running away, that he was the boss, and he gained in confidence every day. This is the secret of the Australian Flat jockeys' method of riding. The jockeys sit into their horses with a tight rein. Instead of being driven, the animal believes that he is getting the better of the argument and tries that much harder. Nicolaus preened himself. He was obviously a very happy horse and looked magnificent with the spring sun shining on his dappled white coat.

They put me on Quick Approach, whom I agreed to ride at Cheltenham. This was a fanatically hard puller, whom I knew by repute in Ireland. When trained by Vincent O'Brien down in Tipperary, he had run away completely out of control and ended up in a haystack, from which he had to be dug out!

At the National Hunt Festival, I had a difficult ride on this horse in the Grand Annual Challenge Cup and, although I never had a chance, I learnt a lot about him which stood me in good stead for the future.

My impression of Nicolaus Silver was correct. He turned

out for the Kim Muir Memorial, an amateur riders' race, ridden by Bill Tellwright, jumped beautifully and won very easily. On the last day I won the Spa Hurdle on Sparkling Flame, but was brought down at the second in the County Hurdle when riding Fulke Walwyn's Roman Sand. It was a heavy fall and I hurt my shoulder, which caused me to miss a ride at Manchester the following day.

However, although it still worried me—shoulders are the most painful things—I was able to take my two rides on Saturday at Hurst Park, an old-established course near Hampton Court, which has now gone the way of Birmingham and Manchester. Here in the George Williamson Chase, I beat David Nicholson on Lord Carnarvon's big high-class young 'chaser, Blessington Esquire, waiting on 'Duke' until coming to the last fence and then pouncing with Scottish Memories to beat him four lengths. In the Triumph Hurdle, Anzio and I were beaten a head by Cantab, ridden with all his tremendous power and skill by Fred Winter, who thus completed a wonderful week in which he had won both the Champion Hurdle and the Gold Cup. John Oaksey wrote about that thrilling finish:

> Bobby Beasley gave not an inch away and was, moreover, suffering very considerable pain from an injury at Cheltenham . . . To us in the stands the result hung on a knife edge all the way to the line—and indeed until the photograph was developed.

I met Anzio again on the eve of the Grand National at Liverpool. He gave me a super ride in the Coronation Hurdle, starting at odds-on and winning easily by six lengths. So I returned to the hotel in great form. But, although that night there was a dinner and dance at the Adelphi and most of the jockeys were there in their dinner-jackets enjoying themselves, I had a quiet dinner and went to bed at nine o'clock, feeling very self-righteous. With the big race tomorrow, I couldn't possibly take part in any celebrations. I thought the jockeys were terrible to do so because I was still a dedicated fitness fanatic, smoking and drinking very little, walking and running a lot.

Nicolaus Silver had only 10 st 1 lb to carry. I did the weight easily with a nice, comfortable 5 lb saddle.

The prize-money for the National had jumped from £13,134 in 1960 to £20,020, easily a record and an extraordinary sum in a sport which still had steeplechases worth less than £200 to the winner. In addition to the organisers, part of the prize was contributed by the Irish Hospital Sweepstakes and part by the mineral firm of Schweppes, who received only seventeen Press mentions for their money and pains, with the result that they transferred their allegiance to their own hurdle race at Newbury. A decision that they have never regretted.

The fences had been altered, chiefly in the hope of attracting top-class 'chasers to Liverpool and, I suppose, partly due to criticism. In the past, many horses had fallen as a result of getting too close to the big upright obstacles. Now they were sloped on the take-off side, giving a horse another yard in which to see the fence and time his take-off. The top weight had been lowered to 12 st.

Automatically on this mark, because they had not run before in England or Ireland, were the two Russian horses, Reljef and Grifel, ridden by B. Ponomarenko and V. Prakhov. So these animals, who were the best steeplechasers in the Iron Curtain countries, but would have been very pushed to win the smallest selling 'chase at Wye, were compelled to give weight to three previous winners—2 lb to the mighty Merryman II, 5 lb to Mr What, and 6 lb to Oxo. There were thirty-five starters.

I hadn't been too keen when I was first booked for Nicolaus Silver and had been tempted to take the ride on Siracusa. And Paddy Sleator hadn't helped matters when he said: 'I thought him a very dear horse when Fred Rimell bought him for 2,600 guineas at Ballsbridge!'

But I had warmed to the grey horse, particularly now that the ground was good and fast, just as he liked it.

We had a nasty scare two days before the race. Fred Rimell's splendid headman, Ron Peachey, reported that the horse had been shod on Thursday ready for the race, but later in the evening they noticed that his left foreleg was swollen and inflamed. 'Then we discovered that a nail had gone in close to the quick. We poulticed his foot, bandaged it, and nursed him throughout that night. On Friday, when we sent him off to Liverpool, he was still not completely sound. It was only a matter of hours before the race that he was given the all clear.'

My father-in-law, Arthur Thompson, was a great help before the race. Among other useful tips, he advised me to keep to the inside all the way if there was no crowding. 'The drops may be bigger,' he said, 'but you should have a clear run, because most of the jockeys will try to stay in the middle for that very reason.' He also told me when to give my horse an easy time and when to ride him hard.

Bryan Marshall, who had also won two Nationals, told me that I was riding too short and advised me to let my stirrup-leathers down about five holes. I followed the advice of both experts and am eternally grateful to them.

There was the same pre-race tension during the preliminaries. Fred Winter was admirably concealing his disappointment at having to ride Ryan Price's new Irish importation, Kilmore, instead of last year's winner, Merryman II, on whom Neville Crump had invited him to deputise for the injured Gerry Scott. Derek Ancil rode the big horse, who was second favourite at 8 to 1 behind the 7 to 1 favourite, Jonjo, the mount of Pat Taaffe. My horse was a 28 to 1 chance, although apparently backed by a number of punters because of his colour. A grey, John's Court, had won the Lincoln, the first leg of the Spring Double.

Before we left the weighing-room, the late Lord Sefton, a tall, handsome, well-built figure with a somewhat pompous, condescending air, warned us all against a mad Charge of the Light Brigade on that long run to the first fence.

That former outstanding amateur rider, John Hislop, then writing for the *Observer*, filed the following copy on that lovely spring afternoon about the race, which was described as the 'Best Grand National for Years':

NICOLAUS SILVER ROMPS IN WITH EARS PRICKED
Aintree, March 25th

1. Nicolaus Silver
         Mr C. Vaughan (T. F. Rimell) 9–10–1
                           H. Beasley   28–1
2. Merryman II
         Miss W. H. S. Wallace (N. Crump) 10–11–12
                           D. Ancil   8–1
3. O'Malley Point
         Mr A. Elliot (W. A. Stephenson) 10–11–4
                           P. A. Farrell   100–6
4. Scottish Flight II
         Mrs A. T. Hodgson (P. Cazalet) 9–10–6
                           W. Rees   100–6

It was a magnificent race for the Grand National, with the grey Nicolaus Silver, owned by Mr C. Vaughan, trained by T. F. Rimell and beautifully ridden by H. Beasley, coming away from last year's winner, Merryman II, who had jumped the final fence with him, to win by five lengths. O'Malley Point was a neck behind the runner-up and just kept Scottish Flight II out of third place, with Kilmore and Wyndburgh close behind.

When the horses came into the paddock the centre of interest was the Russian pair, Reljef and Grifel. Neither looked the part for the job being typical flat-race horses and Reljef, a lightly framed little bay horse, looked barely big and strong enough to jump hurdles.

Both entires, they carried a bloom on their coat which geldings do not have, but neither was well groomed or turned out. With their manes unplaited, tails long and untrimmed, and rawhide bridles, with a circular steel metal disc on the headpiece just below the ears, they had an oriental air about them.

Reljef, who unseated his rider after Valentine's first time round, is a neat little horse, with an attractive, blood-like head, and slightly lop ears. His stable companion, Grifel, is bigger and stronger, but rather plain about the head with a wall eye, a crooked near foreleg and a slight string-halt.

The pick of the field were undoubtedly Merryman II, Scottish Flight II, Nicolaus Silver and O'Malley Point. It is perhaps more than coincidence that these should comprise the first four at the finish, going to show that, though different types of horses often win the National they are almost invariably well made.

The winner, Nicolaus Silver, was one of the most attractive horses in the race. Though lacking the size and scope of Merryman II, and having rather shallow feet, he is a beautifully made, grey gelding, very strong, yet showing plenty of quality. He is compactly built, but standing over a considerable amount of ground and with really good limbs—truly made, with good substance and a particularly straight and powerful hind-leg.

He has a nicely moulded, intelligent head, masculine yet beautiful: a well sloped shoulder, short back and really powerful quarters.

The Russian riders also attracted interest and attention. More heavily built than their English counterparts, especially Prakhov, Grifel's jockey, they presented rather a strange sartorial picture, as they did not wear the usual white neckscarf, used by English riders, nor the elastic bands round the wrists to keep the sleeves of the jacket from flapping about, as a result they looked as if they were wearing pyjama jackets. Ponomarenko, Reljef's jockey, wore a stylish pair of boots, their tops being of white leather with the lower edge generously waved, giving them the appearance of being part of a circus rider's attire.

With the going right on top of the ground, the runners left the gate at a fast pace, but the riders had the sense to steady the speed somewhat after jumping the first couple of obstacles. Spectators were relieved to see the two Russians over safely, but not surprised to see them gradually dropping back to the tail of the field, and soon falling. Prakhov remounted after Grifel had fallen at Becher's first time and continued, finally departing from the race soon after the water on the second round, when a very long way behind. The long lead established by Fresh Winds during the early part of the race was soon cut down, and when the final shape began to form, as it nearly always does after Becher's has been jumped for the second time, there seemed great hopes for a second successive victory for Merryman II, who had survived a kick on his quarters at the post, delivered by Jimuru.

He was going really well in the lead, jumping boldly, accurately and fast, with no sign of weakening. Behind him in a group could be seen Scottish Flight II, Nicolaus Silver, Kilmore, O'Malley Point, Wyndburgh and Mr What. In the clear light, bright but not too sunny, it was a beautiful sight to see these horses sweeping along, a bunch of rhythm and colour.

As the runners headed for the racecourse after jumping the last fence in the country, it was still impossible to say what would win. Merryman II was going as strongly as ever: Nicolaus Silver was moving up ominously: Kilmore, like any horse ridden by the redoubtable Winter, was still a fighting force: while O'Malley Point was creeping up on their heels and Wyndburgh was plugging safely along, ready to take advantage of falls in front of him.

Approaching the last fence, Beasley brought Nicolaus Silver up on Merryman's outside to deliver his final challenge. He took a quick look over his right shoulder to see if there was any danger from that direction and then gave his full attention to getting safely over the obstacle, balancing his horse on landing, and making the best of his way home.

Both horses jumped the fence magnificently, but as they landed it was clear that Nicolaus Silver's advantage in the weight—he was receiving 1 st 11 lb—was bound to tell. Striding away, with his jockey reminding pre-war race-goers of that beautiful and really good rider on the flat, Harry Beasley, father of Nicolaus Silver's jockey, he raced safely home.

Seemingly a little surprised at his splendid isolation, Nicolaus Silver pricked his ears inquisitively about 25 yards from the winning post, but showed no sign of stopping, and in a few strides the race was his.

Merryman II was great in defeat: he battled to the last and only the weight beat him. O'Malley Point stayed a little too well for Scottish Flight II, and age told on Wyndburgh. Kilmore ran a good race but just was not good enough.

The fast going undoubtedly had much to do with the success of Nicolaus Silver. During the early part of the season his form in the mud was poor, but at Cheltenham, on improved ground, he won most impressively and confirmed his liking for these conditions in no uncertain manner yesterday. He is not a great horse—as a race-horse, he is not so fast as his full brother Laird of Montrose—a useful hurdler in his day—but is a great jumper, courageous and stays well.

Moreover he has that not easily defined but essential quality—character. T. F. Rimell, trainer of Nicolaus

Silver, is to be complimented on the horse's appearance and having him trained to the minute.

A footnote which it would be only gracious to include was the courageous and sporting gesture of the Russians to take part, and the fine show put up for a long way by the French amateur rider, M. R. Couetil, who was lying second on Imposant for the first circuit.

And those grand commentators, Clive Graham and Peter O'Sullevan of the *Daily Express* summed up on Monday:

This 1961 Grand inter-National must surely be viewed in retrospect as one of the greatest in the series, re-establishing this Liverpool classic out on its own peak as the top sporting and spectacular event in the world-wide, cross-country racing.

Its links with tradition were emphasised when almost-white Nicolaus Silver beat the 90-year old 'hoodoo' associated with horses of his coat-colour.

And ace-rider 25-year-old H. ('Bobby') Beasley was restoring the family name to the winning role played by his grandfather Harry and brother Tommy when they won four between them in the years 1880–91.

Grandfather Harry rode Come Away (1891) and he won the Grand Sefton five times. Father, also Harry (and formerly first jockey for many years to the late Atty Persse) handled the brilliant Golden Fleece to win the top sprint at the Curragh and the big chase at Leopardstown, all within a few weeks.

Latest in the line, the youngest Beasley has also shown his skill in both spheres by heading the combined list in Ireland.

It was no accident that when seven horses streamed over Valentine's on the second circuit, they were partnered by—not a 'lucky seven'—but seven of the most skilled professionals in the game—Derek Ancil, Fred

Winter, Bobby Beasley, Bill Rees, Paddy Farrell, Pat Taaffe and Tim Brookshaw.

And 'AT BECHER'S ON THE SECOND CIRCUIT THE WINNER MADE HIS FIRST AND ONLY BLUNDER AND WAS DOUBLY FORTUNATE TO FIND HIS RIDER EQUIPPED WITH "AN OLD HEAD ON YOUNG SHOULDERS".'

Yes, that was the only mistake he made. I asked him to stand off a bit far at Becher's the second time, because I was afraid to let him get too close to the fence. I have a photograph of his nose hitting the ground. Any horse less balanced and nimble than Nicolaus would have turned over. He recovered and had taken nothing out of himself. I loved him. Why wouldn't I? He was a very kind, genuine horse, who had jumped with superb precision and given me a great run on the inside all the way. It seemed so easy. It was hard to believe that the dream had finally come true. I had kept up the family tradition. In nine years of racing I was, apart from Fred Winter, the only jockey riding who had completed the big treble, Grand National, Gold Cup and Champion Hurdle. At twenty-five I was on top of the world.

But I remember thinking, as I jumped the last fence, Christ! It's a long way home. That didn't just apply to Aintree.

CHAPTER 9

Stardom

I got tight that night for the first time in my life. The Rimells, Shirley and I were the guests of honour at the fabulous party given by Nicolaus Silver's young owner, Jeremy Vaughan, at the Adelphi. It was a tremendous night. Champagne flowed unlimited. For once, I drank my share and I came out of my shell, let my hair down, relaxed and was in top form like everyone else. It was pure gas. I was just tight enough for that, but I stopped when I thought I'd had enough. I didn't like the idea of getting drunk because I had a horror of not feeling well afterwards.

Halfway through the evening, Fred Rimell took me on one side and asked: 'How would you like to ride as first jockey for me next season? Don't try to decide now. Think it over and I'll be in touch next week.'

I thought of nothing else. All through the week I discussed it with Shirley and Sleator. It didn't seem a very good idea to me because I knew the Irish scene so well and was happy in it, particularly now that I was champion jockey. I think I was frightened to make the change to the big world outside that I didn't know. But Shirley was in favour of a move. She thought I was becoming parochial and, knowing all the aspects of a jockey's life in England, she believed that we would be better off in every way, particularly from the financial point of view. On Easter Saturday, we received the formal offer, which included a retaining fee of £1,000 and a house in Worcestershire. All that before I even started riding. A thousand pounds!

It was like winning the pools. I couldn't believe it. I'd never seen so much money in my life. That for the privilege of riding for such a wonderful stable.

Paddy thought it was a great chance. He was never a man who said much, but I thought he felt that it was a good retainer and I couldn't turn it down. Now he says all would probably have been well had I stayed in Ireland riding for him and remaining champion. We've discussed it at length and he says that, knowing my immaturity and greenness, he was a bit afraid of the effect on me of life in England. He wasn't frightened about the riding, but about the living. And the two were a long way apart. He knew me better than I realised. But, as he had no concrete reason for his fears, he didn't like to voice them. A pity, because I still worshipped him and would have done anything he said.

On the other hand, the success of his horses in England had already formulated in his fertile brain a plan, in which I was to play a vital part.

So I decided to accept. Then on Easter Monday at Fairyhouse's Irish National meeting a telephoned cable was relayed to me in the weighing-room to my acute embarrassment and the delight of all the jockeys and trainers. It was from Fred and was typical of the man. It read: 'CAN YOU RIDE JOE'S GIRL WOORE?' It had to be explained to me that the Rimells had a mare called Joe's Girl and there actually was an English race-meeting called Woore—not Whore!

Anyway, I rode her and she won.

After jumping the Aintree fences it usually takes horses some time to readjust their thinking and timing to ordinary obstacles. But Fred Rimell is the exception to most rules. He put blinkers on Nicolaus Silver, wound him up and we schooled him fast over fences to such effect that only a month after his Liverpool triumph, he ran a tremendous race in the valuable Whitbread Gold Cup at Sandown and, if the going had been on top, I am sure we would have won. As it was, on dead ground, we were second, beaten only four lengths by Dave Dick on Pas Seul.

Kinnersley is a few miles out of the lovely old city of Worcester. Like Paddy Sleator and Grange Con, the Rimells are the village. The house, lying just back off a by-road, is on one side of a short gravelled drive and the yard is on the other. This is not one of your glamour training establishments, but a most attractive old farm, naturally converted, with numerous additions, into a compact, controllable, highly efficient unit. There are hurdles and a loose school, to which Fred owes much of his success, beside the place. The gallops and main schooling ground are across their own flyover on the other side of the busy M5 motorway. There is a modern office, equipped with sumptuous easy-chairs, between the house and the yard. Here, as a matter of routine, we used to meet, with visiting friends or owners, every Sunday morning, discussing the successes and failures of the previous week and our hopes and plans for the week to come. Fred is a most generous host and we always had a glass of champagne by our sides.

At first I was overawed by the whole set-up, which was so different from anything I had ever known. The green boy had arrived in a new world to an amazingly changed status. As a top jockey. I found that I was treated as a friend and an equal by the top people like the Rimells. The same game, but with different trappings and trimmings. Once on a horse, I could live up to my new image of a star in this big league, but, although I tried to assume a sophisticated, man of the world attitude, I was totally unsure of myself. I smoked more to keep my cool and drank upsides with the others to show that I was one of them.

When I turned up to ride out in the morning, I found that my horse had been made ready for me, and, on my return, a lad took the animal off me as a matter of course, while I went home for breakfast, or had it with the Guv'nor and his wife. In the evenings I found we were going out to smart places that I wouldn't have dreamt of going to in Ireland.

Fred had rented us a most attractive thatched house nearby at Birlingham, a lovely old Worcestershire village. We were very happy, particularly when Shirley discovered that she was going to have a baby. Our house was in the village, attached to the greengrocer's shop so there was no difficulty in getting the doctor the day that she fell all the way down the steep old stairs! I was terrified. Luckily all was well, but she developed toxaemia, which was to affect her later on.

Until the season started in England, we went back to Ireland, where we stayed in Wexford with Shirley's parents, who successfully farm about a hundred acres. The skill and Yorkshire thoroughness of Arthur Thompson is much admired by the Irish farmers, who frequently come to him for advice.

I rode a number of winners and won my fourth Galway Plate on Clipador. But, more important, I took a step that summer which I have never regretted and which was, indeed, to prove a life-saver a few years later. With the £2,000 present that I had received after Nicolaus won the National, I bought a small farm of thirty-five acres just up the road from my father-in-law's place at Enniscorthy in County Wexford. It needed doing up, and it seemed a lot of money to Shirley and me at the time; but something prompted me to buy it. I regarded it as an investment against hard times, as, in fact, it turned out to be. It was the best decision I have ever made.

Paddy Sleator was in great form, but rather secretive. 'We'll have an even better time in England this season,' he said. 'I'll bring the horses to *you*.' That sounded all right, but it was several months before I discovered the full extent of his deep-laid plan.

The English jumping season traditionally starts on a quiet

note at the end of July or beginning of August on the Devonshire holiday courses of Newton Abbot and Haldon, which is known as Devon and Exeter. Fred Rimell is one of several trainers who like to take a few horses of the type that come to hand early, and can act on firm going, down to the West Country. The racing contingent stay in one of Torquay's luxury hotels and it's all a big, happy party. It was a revelation to me.

I got friendly with Dave Dick—one of the most tremendous fellows I've ever met. He was the personification of 'gas', prancing round the hotel in his underpants. At this time he was my great hero-figure, a man of the world, a jockey who had lived and done all the things that a real he-man should do. His expensive living never seemed to interfere with his riding. I couldn't understand this and tried to imitate him.

One night we shared a room in Torquay for Newton Abbot races. As a prelude to the night's festivities Dave would lie in the bath, drinking a succession of gin and tonics as he sponged a badly injured leg. After a particularly good night, we went to bed and Dave, out of respect for his leg and the hot weather, slept without clothes or bed-clothes. I woke first in the morning and ordered breakfast, which was brought up by a young Spanish maid. As she walked in at the door, Dave was roused from his slumbers and sat up. In the nude he was quite a sight for a male, let alone a female—like a big gorilla. I don't know whether she thought he was going to pounce on her, but, as soon as this poor girl set eyes on Dave, she dropped the tray and rushed out of the room screaming.

I made a good start as Fred's stable-jockey. We had a useful little hurdler called Jules Verne, who was the ideal sort for Devon, and won three of his first four races. Unfortunately, I found that, apart from Nicolaus Silver, there was an unusually poor lot of horses at Kinnersley that season. Nevertheless such is Fred's skill that he won thirty-five races.

But the new season was barely into its stride when Paddy Sleator announced his bombshell. Feeling that, through lack of opportunity, his good horses were being wasted in Ireland, he rented a stable near Warwick from a small Midlands trainer called Arthur Thomas. Although small in the number of horses that he trained, Thomas was in stature a large, somewhat corpulent man with a round face and a squeaky Birmingham voice. His money and training stables were derived from other business interests: as a sanitary ware merchant, or 'plumbers' provider'.

The Sleator horses lodged with Thomas at Guy's Cliffe, which was, of course, in a splendidly central position for racing all over the country. This was much better than sending them backwards and forwards from Ireland. But, since they could not have two trainers, they were officially described as 'Trained A. Thomas', even though he had nothing to do with them and they were looked after by Paddy's lads from Grange Con.

The first 'Thomas-trained' winner I rode came on October 16 at Hurst Park, where Morland Jack cantered in for the Novice Hurdle, well backed by Sleator and his owner.

At first the Rimells weren't worried. But, as Clipador, Keltie, Scottish Memories, Another Flash and other good horses came over, it became obvious to everyone but me that they were none too happy about the divided loyalty of their stable-jockey. For the time being I had no inkling of the predicament into which I was being plunged, particularly on November 4, when we took Nicolaus Silver back to Aintree and, despite his weight of 11 st 10 lb, won the famous Grand Sefton Chase by two lengths.

But the Sleator horses were very good indeed. A week later at Cheltenham, when I was riding Fred's Icanopit in the Mackeson Gold Cup, Paddy sent over Cathal Finnegan, my successor at Grange Con, to ride Scottish Memories, who won this valuable prize easily—'trained A. Thomas'.

After a lean spell I rode quite a few winners for the Rimells as well as Sleator-Thomas and other outside stables, including Fulke Walwyn, with whom I always got on very well. I found the key to tearaway Quick Approach, the haystack horse. I would let him take charge at the start and then pull him almost right up before the third fence. After that he would be perfectly all right—so much so that I won five good 'chases on him that season. It was riding Quick Approach that taught me the menace (or salutary effect) of TV on a jockey.

I had ridden a bad race at Sandown and was deservedly beaten half a length by Fred Winter on Some Alibi. One of the features of that glorious right-handed racecourse in its natural amphitheatre at Esher, is the famous Pond fence sited on the dog-leg bend into the straight. To save ground you normally jump it at an angle on the inside corner, which was exactly what Fred intended to do as we came into it. But Quick Approach was hanging badly towards the right and I, who should have known better, tried to push my horse up on the inside of Some Alibi. Inevitably Fred jumped into the corner, cutting off my nose and I had to hook up and come on the outside. But for that, I must have won comfortably.

As I rode in, Fred Rimell, one of whose main assets is that he is always forthright and outspoken, gave me the rocket I deserved. However, he is not one to harbour a grudge and, after stopping for a drink on the way home, we were good friends again by the time we arrived back at Kinnersley.

We were met at the door by Mercy. 'I had my beady eye on you,' she said sternly to me. 'What the hell do you mean by trying to come on the inside at the Pond Fence? You would have won otherwise!'

Although it normally goes against the grain with a woman, you can take a rocket from Mercy. She really knows her stuff, does all the entries, bookwork and scheming. A remarkable woman, who still manages to be impeccably, stylishly turned out at all times.

One day that will always stick in my memory was a Saturday in February 1962, when I rode four winners out of the five professional races at Chepstow, including the big one, the T.W.W. Champion Novice Chase, on Paddy's Rupununi, and the four-year-old hurdle on Fred's Pillock's Green.

It was a tremendous day and we all enjoyed a celebration dinner, consuming a fair bit of alcohol. At least I didn't, because I still had this fitness obsession and Mercy is always pretty abstemious. After dinner I was horrified to hear Sleator lecturing Mercy on how she ought to place her horses. She didn't like it one little bit. Why should she when she was just as good at her job as Paddy? Nevertheless, I think that I was more embarrassed than anyone else. I tried to kick Paddy under the table, but he kept on laying down the law and I began to think that I wouldn't be able to continue riding for both stables much longer.

In Ireland I hadn't mixed much with other jockeys, who thought that I was stand-offish. The truth is, I was very shy. My upbringing and environment had helped to make me a loner. In England, away from all the watching eyes in that tight little Irish world, I felt freer to mix and slowly became friendly with a number of my fellow-riders. How vastly different they were from the boys back home. I used to sit, listening to tales of their escapades and watching their antics, which at first shocked, but then amused me greatly.

Superstition has always been rife in racing. For example, Stan Mellor had a quaint way of discovering whether he was going to do well. Before a race he would stand stark naked in the changing-room, slapping his old man against the inside of his thigh. He would not be content unless he achieved the right sounding crack. Failure would make him despondent, but success would mean that he went out for the race, happy and full of confidence. 'That's it! Watch out, you boys, I'll win this one!'

Another very famous jockey, changing beside me one day, had a bandage round his old man. I asked him what had happened. He said: 'Oh, she got a bit wicked and bit me!' A few months earlier, I would have been terribly shocked. Now I thought this was very funny, daring, great gas. And I began to think that, if this sort of thing was all right for these fellows, then it must be OK for me too.

The actual race-riding wasn't nearly as rough as it was in Ireland, where it was the accepted thing to 'do' people and cut them off, put them over the rails or through the wing. I found it was very different in England. If you went to 'do' somebody, he would get very upset afterwards. It wasn't really appreciated. Several times when I first came over, I tried to 'do' David Mould and he didn't like it. I found that, on the whole, it was much easier to ride conventionally and get on with the job of winning instead of wasting time, trying to 'do' people.

There were occasions. David Nicholson at the time appeared to dislike Irish jockeys. When I was riding Scottish Memories in the National Hunt Champion Chase at Cheltenham, 'Duke' kept shouting to George Small, who was on my outside. 'Kill the sod! Kill the Irish bastard! Do him!' But George, a top-class West Country amateur, was a decent chap. He said: 'It's OK, Bobby. Keep coming.'

So I went on all right, but was finally beaten by Dave Dick on Piperton, a fine powerful northern horse with a much longer stride than my chap. In his attempts to 'do' me, 'Duke' obviously didn't realise that I had been brought up on this sort of thing from the time that I first started riding. As Sleator says, 'there's always another day in racing'. It duly arrived for me a short while afterwards in a three-mile 'chase. Coming into the water-jump, I heard someone behind me shouting for room. I looked round and it was David Nicholson. He kept on shouting: 'Bobby, Bobby, a bit of light!' He came up on my inside and I turned him upside down in the water. There was no more trouble after that.

In fact I was now becoming very friendly with most of the lads, particularly Terry Biddlecombe, who lived nearby and was now riding as second jockey to Fred Rimell. A tremendous chap, universally popular, always cheerful, a great horseman and jockey. He possessed those qualities that I had come to admire so much—and still do, for that matter. Tough and hard, gentle and kind. A man, who could play to the limit without his riding suffering in any way. He loved the girls and the girls loved him.

We all liked and respected Fred Winter, already a legend, with that infectious, twinkling smile under the wrinkled hooded eyes, with his fearless determination to win and his essential uprightness, yet always ready to lend a sympathetic ear, or give a helping hand.

The senior jockeys included great gas men like Dave Dick and Tim Brookshaw, while in the younger ranks we had Stan Mellor, who looked as though butter wouldn't melt in his mouth, but was not only an outstanding rider, but a great man on a party, mad for the girls, Josh Gifford, Paul Kelleway, Jeff King and my old friends from Ireland, Willie Robinson and Johnny Lehane. These were just a few in a very happy weighing-room.

We were starting to go to more parties and I was beginning to drink a bit more. At this stage it was having no effect upon me because I was supremely fit and dedicated. It just put me in good form. I was enjoying myself, coming out of my shell and running a little wild in this new exciting world.

I rode Nicolaus Silver again in the National, and I am convinced that, if the going had been on top, he would have won a second time. But heavy rain had turned the ground decidedly soft which, combined with another 9 lb of weight, prevented him from finishing nearer than seventh of thirty-two behind three twelve-year-olds, Kilmore, the mount of Fred Winter, Wyndburgh and Mr What.

On May 26, I rode my last winner of the season in England. I had finished as runner-up in the jockey's championship table to Stan Mellor in front of Fred Winter, Josh Gifford and all the rest. Four days later, Willie Robinson and I both rode winners at Mullingar. I was back with Shirley and our first baby, a girl we called Caroline, in Ireland for the summer.

It had been a splendid first season even though I had suffered a couple of injuries. At Cheltenham in a fall on Magical Way, the cock of the horse's shoe had stabbed through my lower lip, necessitating a few stitches. And Fulke Walwyn's Bigibigi had crashed through the wing at Leicester, knocking my front teeth up into the gums, so that the following day the teeth had to be removed.

I had had my first experiences of the evils of doping, which was the curse of English racing in the early sixties. But for the vigilance of Fred Rimell, they would have got at Nicolaus Silver before the National.

A French girl came round the yard at Kinnersley pretending to be a potential owner. She obviously noted which box Nicolaus was stabled in. But Fred noticed her at Stratford races with some undesirable characters and, prompted by the instinct which makes him a great trainer, swapped Nicolaus with another grey as a precaution. They broke in and got at the other horse all right. All his hair fell out.

During those years favourites were being unaccountably beaten up and down the country. The dopers were no respecters of persons and it was obviously not by any means being perpetrated by just one gang. They broke into the Kent yard of the Royal trainer, Peter Cazalet, and at Newmarket they nobbled the Derby favourite Pinturischio, trained by Noel Murless—twice.

On the Sunday night before Cheltenham they broke into Sleator's yard c/o Arthur Thomas near Warwick and returned to finish their work on Monday, even though the lads were sleeping in the passage with a gun. Six favourites were all beaten and one well-known Irish punter, who is normally very successful lost £80,000.

In his next race after breaking the course record at Hurst Park Morland Jack ran at Ludlow. It was a hair-raising experience. His tongue was hanging out all the way and he smashed every hurdle on the track!

Rupununi was a very good horse indeed—as good as Another Flash or Scottish Memories. But he was never the same animal after being got at before a 'chase at Worcester. I was terrified. He was hot favourite, but he ran as though he was drunk and blind, never jumping a single fence properly.

When they finally caught the Roper gang, I gave evidence at Lewes Assizes and they swore that they'd get me when they came out. I learnt later that they did indeed have a go and missed me by ten minutes.

CHAPTER 10

Celebration

That summer I made the most stupid decision of my life. I decided that, as the interests of my two stables appeared to be clashing, I would leave Fred Rimell and ride as first jockey to Paddy Sleator in England. Today Fred says we could have carried on perfectly well together, that there was no clash of interests and that it was entirely my own idea and decision; but at the time I had convinced myself that he and Mercy resented the Sleator association, and that it was a case of either, or.

He told me that he was collecting a number of better class horses and that, in the long run we should do well. He was, of course, correct. Terry Biddlecombe, who stepped into my shoes at Kinnersley, went steadily up the list until three years later he was champion jockey. So, I suppose, that would have been my lot, all things being equal. And, as I mentioned earlier, unlike some jockeys, who have declared that Fred is difficult to ride for, I have always got on well with him—a tough, but very fair man—and have enjoyed riding for him. I was supremely fit and strong and I have no doubt that the

Rimells, with their vast experience of the pitfalls surrounding a jockey, would have guided me in the right direction.

The Bobby Beasley of today finds it hard to understand the reasons behind that fatal decision. I suppose that, although I was living in England and working for an English trainer, I was still thinking in terms of Ireland and all things Irish. I really hadn't made the break to any marked degree and I had an ingrained loyalty to Ireland and, in particular, to the man to whom I firmly believed I owed so much.

Shirley and I were enjoying a very happy home life. We had no problems about drink or anything else, and she agreed with whatever I wanted to do. Having herself been brought up in racing, she was prepared for changes, and was used to them. It was all part of the game, which was, of course, one of the reasons why I had wanted to marry her in the first place. Yes, it was still a game to me, the one and only, the whole of life—'the incomparable game', as Colin Cowdrey describes cricket. So it never crossed my mind to worry about the drop in the retainer from £1,000 with Fred Rimell, plus that lovely free house in Birlingham and all the other perks, including generous English-style jockey's presents—all in nice crisp tax-free fivers —down to £400 plus the rent of a flat in Leamington and just the 10 per cent of winning prize-money paid by totally taxable cheques. This was all part of the Irish attitude of keeping jockeys in their place and dependent, I suppose. I rode Scottish Memories, for example, in most of his twenty-eight victories, and his Scottish owners, the Sandersons, were charming, generous people. But Paddy insisted that they gave me no more than 10 per cent.

The English trainers were on their jockeys' side. Fred always saw that I got 'readies'. But in Ireland you felt you had to be grateful to the trainer. I remember riding a winner for a trainer who had two cars, a Mercedes and a Volkswagen, who told me that he didn't know how he was going to pay the lads' wages that week. As I wanted to ride the animal again next time, I told him to keep my present, to forget about it. And on another day recently at Navan, when the snow on the ground was balling and conditions were so dangerous that several of the lads didn't want to ride, a trainer came up to me and said: 'You'll ride for me. You're hungry!'

What a crazy fool I was! I turned down a retainer to ride Mill House in all his races from the owner, Bill Gollings, and Sid Dale, then trainer of this magnificent horse, who was to rule the chasing world until he came up against the ruthless brilliance of Arkle. Worse still, on the occasions when I had been prevented through Rimell or Sleator horses from riding for Fulke Walwyn, I had always suggested my old friend, Willie Robinson, as a substitute with good results. That was splendid. But when Fulke asked me to be his stable-jockey, I dillied and dallied instead of accepting at once, as, of course, I should have done. Then I had a crashing fall at Stratford and, by the time that I had sorted out my ideas a few weeks later, it was too late. Naturally fed up with waiting for my answer, Fulke had offered the job to Willie, who accepted gratefully and started a highly successful, profitable partnership.

All this out of a strange, twisted Irish loyalty to Sleator, which he had never demanded. Make no mistake. It wasn't Paddy's fault.

So we moved to Leamington Spa, a smallish busy Midlands town near Warwick, handily situated for Guy's Cliffe, where the Sleator horses were lodged.

It was an extraordinary set-up, run, through remote control, by Paddy on the telephone from Grange Con. Arthur Thomas received little money from Paddy. He revelled in the publicity he was given as the ostensible trainer. He held the licence, but had nothing at all to do with the horses, which were prepared by Paddy in Ireland and sent over ready to run in races, which the Guv'nor, in consultation with me, had selected. Thomas had a few horses in his own yard and never came into ours.

Jim Leigh, the headman, and I organised everything. Jim was a brilliant man, a typical product of Ireland, possessed of the same dedication to the horses and the game as myself.

Nothing else mattered, least of all his wage which was much lower than that of most of his English counterparts. He worked tremendously hard and inspired the excellent Irish stable-lads, whom we had imported from home. It was very much a straight transfer of Grange Con to England.

Arthur received a lot of press coverage for his 'all-weather gallops', which were claimed to provide perfect going in all conditions. In fact the Ford foundry at Leamington, where they made, I think, radiators, paid Arthur half-a-crown a ton to dump their waste at Guy's Cliffe and the gallops were made of dry ground metal filings. When it was wet, you would come in from riding exercise black all over. The stuff used to get in your eyes, teeth, nose, ears and the horses had to be hosed down. Moreover, rolling compressed the stuff into a solid metal base so that, when it rained, there was no cushion, as you might have expected if you inspected them in dry weather. When there was a hard frost, Jim Leigh had to go out at two in the morning to harrow the gallops. You should have seen what was unearthed: bits of iron, brick and other assorted debris calculated to harm a horse's legs.

Whereas I had 335 mounts and sixty-five winners in my Rimell season, I dropped down to seventh position with 220 rides and only thirty-five winners. I missed the bread and butter riding fees and, of course, the presents, although I was so irresponsible that this had not started to worry me at all yet. Mind, I had gone from quantity to quality. We had some wonderful horses, including Scottish Memories, Another Flash, Forgotten Dreams, Rupununi and San Jacinto. Hand-picked horses, trained to perfection by a brilliant trainer, all ready when they arrived, winning big and small races, usually on a Saturday. One season we had eighty-six runners, forty winners and as many placed. We were unique in British racing and the punters' delight—that is, all the public punters, but not Arthur Thomas, in whose name they ran.

I said that Arthur revelled in the publicity. He did. After a winner you would see him squeaking away to the Press, giving them the horse's future plans, blissfully unaware that they were all wrong, while Paddy, saying nothing, leant against a wall or rail in the background, smiling that half-smile and pensively puffing away at the cigarette-holder. 'Come on, Bobbee,' Arthur would say. 'We're going to make some money this season. You tell me all about them and I'll have a good bet. Then, when they win, I can give you really good presents.'

Once again I was a complete idiot, because he would have been as good as his word and I could have made a nice nest-egg. Instead I thought only of Sleator, who told Jim and me never to tell Arthur anything. On the contrary I, who had the unenviable job of 'pig-in-the-middle' between Sleator and Thomas, was instructed to 'put him away'—give him false information—so that Paddy and his owners could get a decent price.

So there were some terrible scenes during the five years that this strange association lasted. One day a ten-year-old horse came over from Ireland. He had pretty good form, but had never run over fences, but he was entered up in 'chases. On the way to the races, Arthur always tried to pump me for information. 'Will 'e win, Bobbee? 'e must 'ave a good chance, eh, Bobbee?'

I put him away, telling him that the horse was too old and set in his ways and was unlikely to jump a big English steeple-chase course. Needless to say, Paddy had a good bet and the old horse cantered in at 10 to 1. Arthur accepted my delighted surprise and was not unduly upset as he drove me back to Guy's Cliffe.

Driving with Arthur was one of the worst occupational hazards of this job. From the moment that we left the yard he fought a constant verbal and physical running battle with every other user of the road, screaming and cursing at them in his shrill broad Birmingham accent.

A week later I made more excuses for the animal. It was his first handicap and he was too much of a novice to jump well against these very experienced rivals. He jumped beautifully and won as he liked. Arthur was not best pleased as we drove home. 'I'm beginning to think you're putting me away, Bobbee,' he said, with amazing intuition.

The horse's third outing was a 3½-mile 'chase at that charming little Welsh course Bangor-on-Dee. I told Arthur that he wouldn't like the heavy ground and that he was most unlikely to stand up, let alone get the trip in those conditions. Revelling in it like the true mudlark that he was, the old horse trotted up again.

This time Arthur went mad, screaming at me: 'You fucking Irish bastard! I'm going to run you back to your potato patch in the bog!' In his anger he almost ran me over in the car park and then drove off, leaving me to find my own way back to Leamington. I had a much more pleasant lift home.

When I went up to Guy's Cliffe next day, Arthur was still in a tearing, screaming rage. He'd missed three good winners. He was going to run me off the place. I was to get out and never come back. It was such a performance, that Paddy had to come over from Ireland to cool him down and make the peace.

Of course Arthur had no idea of the value of Irish form. San Jacinto, a five-year-old, came over, having just won two very high-class bumpers at Limerick Junction and Leopardstown in impressive style. He was entered for the Gorsebrook Novices' Hurdle at Wolverhampton. This time, although Arthur never believed us, we didn't put him away. Paddy had told me to give him a nice, quiet introductory race, as the owners were away on a cruise and he was going to be a good horse. He started at 100 to 9 and ran so freely, that I don't believe I could have stopped him even if I'd wanted to. He made all the running, smashing every hurdle on the track, uprooted the last clean out of the ground and beat the odds-on favourite by four lengths in a common canter. That time I was equally unpopular with Sleator and Thomas.

Only some of our Irish lads and our loyal local followers made money out of that race, and they did very well indeed.

An Irish barber in Leamington, who used to follow our horses, earned enough to redecorate his shop. And an Italian wine waiter at the Saxon Mill Hotel next door to Guy's Cliffe, influenced no doubt by the horse's name, made a tidy sum. A few years later, I had a splendid meal in the restaurant that he had bought with the money he won on our horses.

Then there was the big gamble at Nottingham. Not only Arthur, but everyone else had to be kept strictly in the dark. Shirley and I went to the races early and I sent her up into the stands to hide, so that nobody would ask her to tell them whether the horse was fancied or not. Although he hadn't much form in Ireland, I knew that he was supposed to be a really good thing. He won like it and I learnt afterwards that Paddy and his owners had made about £8,500. I got £13 for winning on him and nobody would talk to me for quite a while afterwards!

More screams from Arthur. I must say there were times when I felt very sorry for him. But then, after all, there was no need for him to keep this bogus association going. Because, after all, it *was* bogus and, although I was too naïve and blind to see it, it caused a great deal of justified resentment, first among other English trainers, and then among the powers that be. It was bound to end in tears. Although the Rules of Racing were not being broken—Paddy was far too cute for that—they were being bent. In a business like racing, where things, involving thousands of pounds, can so easily go wrong, the Jockey Club must have one man who is ultimately responsible for each individual horse—the trainer. But in this case, the real trainer was living in Southern Ireland, out of their jurisdiction, and the man, whom they licensed as the trainer, had nothing whatever to do with the horses. If there had been any hanky-panky, Arthur would have carried the can even though he would have been quite innocent. In retrospect, it is amazing that it lasted until 1967. And I blame the authorities for not having the courage to tell Paddy that the arrangement was unsatisfactory and must stop. This could have been accomplished in

the friendliest possible way through their friends and counterparts in Ireland, so that no eggs would have been broken. But
it appears that commonsense and ordinary human feelings were
singularly lacking in the Jockey Club and National Hunt
Committee at that time.

I often wonder how we managed to keep the horses sound
at Guy's Cliffe. In fact it was very difficult. We were always
worrying that they would injure themselves. Apart from all the
foreign bodies in the foundry waste, there was no rail or any
other method of keeping horses in if they failed to turn sharply
on the bottom gallop. One animal actually went into the river!
But Jim Leigh and our half-dozen lads were wonderful. They
all pulled their weight and made a happy harmonious team.
Three of them are now training in England or Ireland. Jim
has a string near Gainsborough in Lincolnshire.

Shirley was a tremendous help. Although she soon had
another child, our son, Peter, to look after, she booked my
rides with such success that, even in 1966–7, the last season
before the break-up of the Sleator-Thomas partnership, I rode
thirty-four winners from 236 mounts and finished tenth on the
list. Indeed, during those years I was seventh, eleventh,
seventh, fourth and tenth in that order. And, I was averaging
about 250 rides a season, which allowed us to live in fair
comfort.

Our marriage seemed to be prospering in every way,
although I was far too wrapped up in racing and myself to be
a good husband and father.

There were a few injuries. One evening meeting at Uttoxeter,
I dislocated my shoulder. It had to be put back immediately
and the racecourse doctor was doing his best when Johnny
Lehane came into the ambulance room. 'Hold on fruit,' he said,
as he saw my grey, agonized face. 'I'll get you something for
it.' He ran out and returned with a whole bottle of whisky,
which he proceeded to pour down my throat. Then, seeing that
the doctor was still struggling, he handed the bottle to him.
'Come on, doc. We haven't all night. I reckon you need it

more than Bobby!' Sure enough it did the trick and the doctor, well fortified, found the necessary extra strength to force the shoulder back into place.

Poor Johnny, another immature Irishman who, hopelessly depressed through pills and alcohol, was later to take his own life—inadvertently, because, as so often happens, he was convinced that he would be discovered and saved before the fatal drugs took effect. I found him one day down at the start of a novice 'chase, giving his horse a fair old hiding. 'Stop it!' I said. 'Why the hell are you doing that?' Johnny grinned. 'I'd rather frighten them before they frighten me!' he replied.

Half-way through this period a stone hit my left eye during a race at Nottingham. I took no notice of it until the next day, when I was cantering down to the start at Windsor and found that I was seeing two hurdles on top of each other and two sets of rails at an angle. I didn't know what on earth was happening, tried closing one eye and found that was all right. The other jockeys suggested goggles with a bit of plaster half over the left eye. This worked well until the goggles misted up, as I was coming down the hill at Cheltenham on a frosty day with glaring sun. I couldn't see the last at all. So I pulled them down and closed one eye, but found that I still couldn't judge my approach or tell my horse when to take off. Luckily he was good enough to take off on his own and I went on and won. But that was too much. I went straight up to a specialist in London, who gave me tests and at first suggested an operation on the damaged retina. Then he decided that it was best to leave it alone. He tried a special pair of glasses in an attempt to pull the retina which had become lazy. Eventually, however, he told me that I would have to learn to live with this double vision. Another jockey who had the same trouble advised me to keep my head more upright when I was riding. This helped.

At the end of November 1964, I was enjoying a tremendous run of success—twelve winners in a row, including a treble at Haydock—when I had a crashing fall on Milo in a 'chase at Worcester and broke my nose badly. Worcester Infirmary

could do nothing. Back at Leamington there was no chance of
an operation because the surgeon was away and the matron
said that I might have to wait for at least a week until he
returned. I was desperate, because five days later I was due
to ride a brilliant new novice called Moonduster for Paddy
Sleator at Liverpool. Bryan Marshall suggested the London
Clinic, but it would cost me a fair bit. 'Hang the expense!'
said the dashing Beasley.

I telephoned the Clinic. 'Come up on Monday,' they said,
'and we'll operate.' A beefy barman, called Phil Hertz, who
weighed 17 st despite a peg-leg, and used his car as a part-
time taxi, drove me up to London, where they operated on my
nose. It took four hours and the next day I was full of
anaesthetic and feeling desperate. They told me that I would
have to remain in bed for at least another four days. So I
discharged myself, went back to Leamington and then drove
up to Liverpool, feeling distinctly woozy.

I knew very little about the race. Moonduster was 15 to 8
favourite in a big field. I was so weak that he ran away with
me, but we won easily by five lengths. I didn't even remember
pulling up and, after I had weighed in, I passed out. The
nurses at the Clinic, who couldn't believe it, sent me tele-
grams of congratulation.

The operation cost me £180 and I received just a £20
cheque for winning. But I'd won and I didn't give a damn.
That was what life was all about.

I rode Nicolaus in one more National, but he had started
to break blood-vessels. His racing career was over. How I
loved that horse! Some time later I met a girl near Newbury,
who said she had him as a hunter. I tried to buy him to give
him a good home in Ireland for the rest of his life, but she
refused. The next week he broke a leg out hunting and had to
be put down.

My word, those Sleator-Thomas horses were good. No
wonder other people became jealous. In the 1965–6 season
Black Ice won seven races, finishing with the four-year-old

championship, the Daily Express Triumph Hurdle at Cheltenham.

I've written about wonderful Scottish Memories and his twenty-eight victories without ever feeling the whip once.

Despite his short back, Another Flash was nearly as good a 'chaser as he was over hurdles. There was a lot of grief in the last Mackeson Gold Cup run at Wetherby, but despite considerable interference through the race, we were going to win. I let him come too fast into the last fence, so that he hurdled it and fell. God, I was upset. I thought he was dead when he lay there unconscious for a good five minutes. A week later he won a condition hurdle at Windsor with his ears pricked. He was first, second and third in the Champion Hurdle. The year he finished second to Magic Court, the going was far too soft for him and he had been laid off for twelve months with desperate enteritis.

Rupununi shrugged off his doping but he was brought down in the Mackeson Hurdle at Cheltenham. Half a dozen horses galloped over him and kicked him badly. Thereafter he lost his confidence and was nervous and windy, although he still managed to win races. But a piece of that foundry iron at Guy's Cliffe ran right up into his foot and drained out all the hoof oil so that he had to be put down.

During the icy English winters, I found that, through thin racing breeches, I was often suffering from freezing cold in a most embarrassing place. It was agony and I had visions of it dropping off. So Shirley knitted me a sort of angora finger, which I wore when I was riding in those conditions. Most comfortable, except when I was taken short and found it hard to get off in a hurry! This gave the jockeys a good laugh.

What fun it all was. I was now an established leading jockey and accepted as one of the boys. Away from the racecourse we had so many lovely parties. As I was going around so much with Terry Biddlecombe, who has always loved champagne, it seemed only natural for me to drink it too. I quite liked champagne, but I have never enjoyed any other alcoholic drink for the taste. But I began to like the effect. As the others got merry, so did I. Under the Press stand at Cheltenham, there is a little cellar bar, reserved for trainers and jockeys. We would all gather there and drink champagne after racing. Then, on the way home, we'd probably stop at a pub and have a few more. Sometimes I'd end up a little the worse for wear and suffer from a slight hangover the next morning. But drink had no effect on me. I was riding as well as, if not better than, ever before. I didn't become vicious or resentful when I drank. Things were going well and this was a new life, great gas. I had seen this life from the outside and now I was inside it. This would do me no harm. This was living. And I rode out early every morning as fit and as fresh as ever.

In November 1963, I drank plenty of champagne at the annual Champion Jockey's dinner in Cheltenham. I ate nothing because I was watching my weight and I finished the evening, like most of the other jockeys, fairly merry. The next morning I quickly dispelled my hangover with another glass of champagne and arrived at the course, feeling right on top of the world.

I was riding Fulke Walwyn's second string, the grey Richard of Bordeaux in the biggest race so far of the new English jumping season, the £5,000 Mackeson Gold Cup, run over two miles. Willy Robinson, as Fulke's stable-jockey, was on the better fancied Some Alibi, but mine was a 20 to 1 outsider in this field of twenty high-class 'chasers. I rode one of the finest races of my life.

John Oaksey wrote in the *Sunday Telegraph*:

Jumping, if Fulke Walwyn will pardon the expression, like a particularly determined cat, Mr Jack Schilizzi's Richard of Bordeaux led almost from start to finish to win the Mackeson Gold Cup here today.

He was in fact the 'neglected' from Walwyn's apparently invincible yard—and Some Alibi, ridden by the stable jockey Willie Robinson finished far behind.

But the Walwyn luck continues—with £17,500 already in the bag and Mill House still to come.

An elegant, even fastidious grey who does not much care for mud in his face, Richard of Bordeaux went straight to the front today—and thereafter the only horse he or his rider Bobby Beasley ever saw was the tearaway Irishman One Seven Seven.

And as the two sailed away, jumping stride for stride, the opposition had already begun to thin out. As Piperton and Corrigadillisk fell at the first, Fortria blundered horribly beside them.

Until the last fence of all it was his only mistake—but as Pat Taaffe said later they were always going just too fast for him.

Plenty fast enough it seemed, for most of the others. Strung out like routed cavalry behind the leading pair nothing had even begun to close the gap turning down the final hill. Although two fences from home One Seven Seven was clearly feeling the strain Richard of Bordeaux galloped on relentless and untiring.

Between the last two Blue Dolphin giving it all as usual, struggled out of the pack in pursuit—but might just as well have chased a moonbeam.

Flicking cleanly after the last Richard of Bordeaux showed him no trace of mercy up the hill and at the post Blue Dolphin was still four lengths behind. Ten lengths away Too Slow was third, Mariner's Delight was fourth and Fortria fifth.

What John didn't know, perhaps, was that down at the gate I kept saying to the lads: 'I'm going on like the clappers. Don't take any notice of me. I'll come back to you.' They thought I was out for a bit of gas, and that I was only there to make the running for Some Alibi.

So I jumped off into the lead, with Tommy Carberry on

One-Seven Seven hanging on for dear life. My horse was jumping superbly and felt inspired. I was asking him way off every fence and he was giving me everything. At the top of the hill, I opened up the lead again and the lads realised too late that I wasn't coming back to them. I'd put one over on them and we had a rare old celebration in the cellar-bar that Saturday evening.

As time went on I discovered that there was more to this business of riding in England than met the eye. I was getting quite a few rides for a trainer who had a lot of horses and a sexy sort of wife. I had been riding for her on the first day of a two-day meeting near her house. Her husband was away and she invited me to stay the night. I refused because I had to get back to work Another Flash in the morning. She did her best to persuade me but I held out and went home. I was not employed by that stable again. Another jockey was riding their horses. Perhaps he stayed overnight.

During the summers in Ireland I enjoyed quite a bit of success for Phonsie O'Brien, younger brother of the great Vincent, and Kevin Bell. Some of the Irish jockeys seemed determined to do me now that I was one of the leading lads in England. Johnny Crowley, for one, kept having a go until the day that, sensing he was behind me on the rails approaching a fence, I eased my horse back so that he was held there with his animal's head inside my horse's quarters. If I had moved, he would deservedly have been through the wing. But I stayed on a straight course and, as we pulled up, I asked him: 'Johnny, what would have happened . . .?' He looked down. 'All right,' he said. 'I know. We'll call it a day.' It was all quite unreasonable, but just part of the Irish scene.

Another jockey was determined to do me one day at Thurles when I was riding for Kevin Bell. Everywhere I went he followed. Then he had a real go and came straight at me. I accelerated out of the way, but he was going so fast he couldn't stop. He missed me and hit another horse, nearly cutting its leg off. Not only was he promptly given a rare whipping by the injured horse's rider, but, when he got back, he was summoned by the stewards and suspended for a month.

I was had in twice by the stewards. On one occasion at Leopardstown, I might have won had an American champion jockey, enjoying a busman's holiday in Ireland, not come right across me at the last hurdle, nearly bringing me down. I objected, as was only fair to my owner and trainer, but was fined £20 by the stewards for a frivolous objection. 'What are you trying to do to this guest of ours?' they demanded.

But I thoroughly deserved one reprimand through not keeping my wits about me. Having ridden in the previous race at Limerick Junction, I went to the scales to weigh out for the next in breeches and singlet with the colours over my arm and was reported to the stewards by the Clerk of the Scales for being 'indecently dressed'.

When summoned into the presence, I explained that we always did this in England. The senior steward looked up. 'Do you, Beasley?' he asked. Like a fool, I hadn't noticed that it was Evan Williams, who was now a Master of Foxhounds in Ireland, but had been a top-class pre-war professional jumping jockey in England, winning the 1937 Grand National on Royal Mail!

Now I was drinking my share all the time in Ireland. No one noticed. It was expected of me because it's a way of life over there. They would only have been upset had I refused to drink with them.

They regarded me as I regarded myself—a leading jockey, a man of the world, a hard man, who loved gas and any excuse for celebrating with a 'jar'.

CHAPTER 11

Dissipation

I had so many friends in England now, that I didn't miss
Shirley as much as I should have done when she stayed over
with her parents in Ireland for one reason or another, like
having a baby. I was learning fast about the other side of a
jockey's life.

One cold day a number of jockeys, myself included, set off
for Lingfield by train only to learn, when we were half-way
there, that the meeting had been abandoned because of frost
in the ground. Racing was due to start early at that time of the
winter, and by 10.30 a.m. we were all back in London, meeting
by arrangement in the famous Jermyn Street Turkish baths.
Soon someone ordered twenty bottles of champagne. By lunch-
time we were all getting as high as kites and at about three
o'clock somebody said: 'Time for birds, lads.' He got on the
telephone and said: 'It's organised. We've got to go to so-and-
so.' We piled into three taxis. On arrival at our destination,
we went up to a large flat, where there were several birds. The
other lads went off to enjoy themselves together with one or
two of the girls, but Stan Mellor and I stayed behind, talking
and drinking with two other birds. 'Aren't you going to

have . . .?' they asked us. 'No,' we said. 'No.' Stan, as I have written, is a very natural fellow in every way and I know that even I, full of champagne, would have had a right go if I had been on my own, away from the crowd. But the thought of communal sex was too much for me. I couldn't let the others see what I was doing. So we sat there until they returned happily chatting about their exploits. We all had a bit more to drink before leaving for Paddington and home. I started congratulating myself on being so good, but realised this was hypocritical. I still had a built-in feeling that it was sinful and I wasn't going to let others see me sinning. Besides, Stan and I were both married. It puzzled me that none of the jockeys paid anything for their sexual adventures. I was soon to learn the reason.

I had had that telephone call about stopping Another Flash in the Champion, but had not been worried again until the Sleator-Thomas horses started carrying all before them. Then the calls started. They came mainly from bookmakers and some from a few individual big punters. All the telephone calls were propositions for information and there seemed to be a recognised fee, £500. The message was always the same. I would receive £500 in readies by registered post the next day if I would say whether the horse I was riding tomorrow was fancied or not. In racing parlance, whether it was 'off', having a real go.

I knew some of the callers by sight and had even been intro-duced to a few of them. Others were new names. I always refused to give them any information not only out of loyalty to Sleator, but also for fear of where it might lead. I was never asked to stop one at that stage. They just wanted the informa-tion and were prepared to pay handsomely for it. It would have been so easy to make a pile of money with little or no risk of it ever coming to light. And, although there's an old rule of racing saying that you mustn't sell information, it would have been very hard to prove that you had been doing anything wrong. I've often wondered how many of my fellow jockeys gave the information requested by those callers and prospered accordingly.

Not that Shirley and I didn't need the money badly. We'd bought ourselves a nice house in Leamington and had the devil of a job to find the mortgage.

Then there were the night-clubs and the 'birdmen'. On the fringe of racing, ingratiating themselves with leading jockeys and some trainers, there exists a motley tribe of hangers-on who are mostly well in with bookmakers. They are plausible spivs of varying means and status, living on their wits in constant hope of gleaning rewarding pieces of information. If asked to describe themselves, they would say they were professional punters. All the ones I met seemed to have free access to night-clubs as well as many ravishing girls at their beck and call.

My first experience was an eye-opener. Another jockey had introduced me to a man who knew the London scene well and was apparently a punter-cum-birdman. My horses were all winning. I was on the crest of the wave and he knew it. He must also have known that I was a proper greenhorn. I heard the lads talking about this other, exciting world, and I was obsessed with the desire to get involved in it.

So, when this chap telephoned me at home, I was at once thrilled and frightened. 'I'm coming to Stratford,' he said. 'I've got two ravers with me. You're riding hard and you need a bit of relaxation. How would you like a good night, a bit of gas, eh?'

I thought to myself this is wrong, but I can't resist it. So I said: 'OK. I'll see you in Stratford at half-past eight.'

After a few drinks I conquered my terrible conscience, and went out and met him as arranged. He hadn't exaggerated. The two girls with him were proper ravers, really lovely, smashing young birds whom he'd brought down from London. He gave us a champagne dinner in a little, expensive restaurant in Stratford, during which the old dedication hammered in my head: 'You're riding at Chepstow tomorrow. This is wrong. It's madness.'

But when I saw that one of those gorgeous girls was wearing nothing but a short skirt under her smart fur coat and I felt the warming effect of the liqueur brandy on top of the wine, my resistance disappeared and I decided to chance it. It didn't seem to affect the others at all, and I was every bit as good as them, wasn't I?

Fool that I was, I didn't realise that my generous host was only doing this in order to get information. He was much older than I was and obviously wise to my weakness. We walked back to a hotel and went up to a large double room with a bathroom and another bedroom adjoining. He ordered several bottles of champagne. Soon I was in a fair old state of excitement and, when the girl, who was full of fun, removed her fur coat, sat on my knee and started to make a fuss of me with no holds barred, I thought that at last I was making up for all those sterile years in Ireland.

The punter and the other girl discreetly slipped out into the next room, leaving us alone together. She undressed me and took off her skirt, giving me time to admire her sensational, firm young body before she got into bed beside me. Then for five hours she did everything to me, breaking down all my inhibitions and far exceeding my wildest dreams. I was young and fit, there was more champagne by the bed. I responded fervently and we were ecstatically happy. I remember she loved the contrast of her hair, which was dark and mine, which was fair. We never slept. It was still dark when our host came in, opened another bottle and suggested that we'd better be going. He asked nonchalantly whether my horse at Chepstow was fancied. I said: 'I think I've got a bit of a chance. That is if there's anything left of me!'

So I went home in a state of blissful euphoria, thinking that I'd done wrong, but that, by God, it was worth it; bathed, shaved, changed and set off for Chepstow. That beautiful, green undulating racecourse amidst the hills of the Wye valley seemed the same as ever, but I was a different man now. I was sure I wouldn't be able to ride as well. In the changing-room the lads chaffed me because I was so quiet and I couldn't stop blushing with a sheepish sort of smile, while pretending to be the big, tough, dashing man of the world.

I was still day-dreaming as I was put up on my horse and led round the parade-ring. Unlike some jockeys, I normally listen to the lad as he prattles on at this time, seizing his one opportunity of telling me of the horse's peculiarities and how, in his opinion, it should be ridden. After all he's with the horse every day, in and out of its stable, and I've often picked up valuable hints about individual animals in this way. But today I was oblivious of him and of the crowds on the paddock rails, when suddenly a voice said: 'Hallo, my golden prick. Good luck now!' There, leaning on the rails in her fur coat was the bird with whom I'd spent the night. I forced a smile and just cringed in the saddle as all the guilt feelings came flooding back. Jesus, what had I done? Where had I been? Where the hell was I going? I daren't go round again past her. So I made the boy lead straight out on to the track and, as I cantered down, feeling the horse strong beneath me, my head cleared and I dismissed these thoughts. There was a job to be done, my own special job that I knew better than most. I'd show them what a hard man could do. So I rode a tremendous race with one of my famous 'power-packed' finishes and won by a short head.

I never saw that girl again, but there were plenty more from the same source. The punter realised that I had never seen any life, and had no experience of sex. He believed he was sure to get some information if he kept plying me with birds and booze.

When things are going well, you are surrounded with friends. Those same friends are apt to disappear in bad times. But I hasten to add that a few of the punters are naturally generous and will still do anything to help even when a chap is down on his luck. Two such men were the late Monty Cosky and Jimmy the Spiv, an entertaining, immaculately groomed sort of chap, whom I still meet on the rare occasions I go racing in England nowadays.

I got to know another man in London, who had considerable contacts and introduced me to the night-clubs. A lot of the jockeys were involved. It was the 'in scene'. Those brought up in England took it all for granted. To me it was a new experience. I had never seen it before and didn't know how to cope with it After the first day of a two-day meeting at one of the 'Park' courses—Lingfield, Sandown, Kempton or Ascot—it seemed natural not to go back to Leamington, but to stay the night in London. As a jockey's daughter, Shirley understood this and didn't expect me to come all the way home. I would stay with this punter, who would take me out to glamorous, softly-lit night-clubs, where I often met the other lads. He would produce a beautiful bird for me and give us a slap-up dinner with quantities of champagne, for which I was developing an extraordinary liking. I couldn't get enough of this life. I began to feel that I was a great fellow, a real man, getting well pissed, the life and soul of the party, waking up in the morning with yet another bird and immediately ordering champagne without ever having to pay a penny. I was still so fit, that I was able to throw off my hangovers, but I was finding drink in the morning a necessity to put me back in good form again. I didn't know what was happening to me. And at this stage I didn't care.

Life was one long party. I was starting to drink at home now—not a lot but quite openly—and got quite annoyed when Shirley refused to join me. She never has been more than just a social drinker.

One of the nastiest experiences for any horseman, is when a horse dies under you. Paddy Sleator sent over a top-class Irish chaser called Billy Bumps. He ran second to Arkle at Cheltenham and then ran again against the great horse at the National Hunt Festival. He looked a stone-cold certainty in a chase at Bangor-on-Dee until, leading at the second last fence, his heart gave out and he fell with me like a ton of bricks.

Some time later, I rode the Engelhard horse, Right Noble, who had been favourite for the Derby, ridden by Lester Piggott. He developed a habit of hanging very badly, and they thought he was becoming a rogue on the flat. So he went jumping and showed a lot of promise. I rode him at Sandown in a novices' hurdle. We were six lengths in front coming to the last, when he crashed down with a terrifying thump. The vet said he was dead before he hit the ground.

On the way back from Newton Abbot one evening several of us stopped for the night at a hotel, where, owing to shortage of accommodation, I shared a bed with a great friend, a famous jockey, who was always having trouble with his weight and was 'wasting' with the help of 'piss-pills', devastating saluric pills which dry you out and thus counteract your drinking.

We had had a heavy night on champagne before we retired to bed. Suddenly there was a knock on the door, and a girl, who was mad about my glamorous unmarried friend, came through on her way back to her room from the bathroom. 'Come on into bed', said he, seizing her and pulling her unresisting in between us. He started to make love to her, but the booze and the pills combined to ruin his performance. Eventually, exhausted, he said: 'Hell, it won't work!' and collapsed fast asleep.

I lay as still as a mouse for a while. Then I said quietly: 'I hate to see a lovely girl like you so frustrated. Do you think that perhaps I'd have a bit of a squeak?' We enjoyed ourselves all through a wonderful night and, when she left at dawn, my friend was still asleep. He hadn't the slightest idea what had been happening beside him.

I said earlier that Monty Cosky, who used to bet for several trainers, was a very generous little man. One day I met him in London, where I had arranged to spend the night with a certain young, very attractive married woman at a most expensive hotel. 'Having a night out, are you, my boy?' he asked. 'You'll probably need this.' He handed me £30 in readies and wouldn't hear a word of refusal.

It is strange how these punters offer girls in the same way that another man offers a drink. Two nights before he died Monty met a teetotal friend of mine having dinner in a big hotel at Nottingham. He was worried. 'What can I give you, my boy?' he said. 'It's no good offering you a drink, I know. Would you like a girl? There's a beautiful bird in my room right now. She's got a lovely body, a dancer. The boys are going through her up there. She's yours for nothing if you want to join in. Have her on me.'

My friend gratefully declined, saying that he would always rather open the batting than go in third wicket down and accepted a cigar instead.

Among the high spots of this heady period, I had the great honour of riding the Queen Mother's 100th winner on Gay Record in the Sevenoaks Chase at Folkestone. It was a tremendous thrill for me, an Irishman, which I will never forget. I was lucky enough to ride several more winners, including the high-class French horse, Worcran, for the most popular owner in racing.

Indeed, as I look back through the cuttings books, and see all the big race victories at the top courses, earning headlines such as 'Beasley continues fantastic sequence', 'Brilliant Beasley', etc. I certainly had cause to celebrate, and it is small wonder that I thought it would go on for ever.

CHAPTER 12

Disillusionment—the Harder They Fall

After five years of unbroken success, in 1967 the end came suddenly—and without warning.

Of course we had known that there was jealousy and resentment of the Sleator-Thomas set-up, but as the turf authorities had allowed it to carry on for all that time, it is hard to see how they justified breaking it up with no thought at all for those involved. If they were going to stop it, the time for that was surely at the beginning. I, for one, had never done anything to be ashamed of on the racecourse and had never fallen foul of the stewards in England or Ireland.

The break-up was engineered in an extraordinary way. Arthur Thomas was up at a Northern meeting, saddling one of his own small string, which was being ridden by an amateur. Outside the weighing-room, in full view of everyone, Arthur's owner was handing his jockey his travelling expenses for coming all the way up from the Midlands to Scotland. It was all perfectly legitimate. But a stipendiary steward reported Arthur for paying money to an amateur. Ignoring his protests, they took way his licence to train and informed him that he would get it back only when all Paddy Sleator's horses were removed from Guy's Cliffe.

Suddenly the bottom had fallen out of my world. Paddy tried to get round it. Toby Balding offered us a yard at Weyhill and it was suggested that Jim Leigh could hold the licence. No. The English and Irish authorities ruled that the only way in which Sleator horses could be trained in England was if Paddy left Ireland to hold the licence himself, which, of course he was not prepared to do. They said he couldn't train in two places at once. He had to be in command on the spot.

So I watched the lads and the horses all leaving for Ireland and I walked round that empty yard weeping tears of frustration. Strangely I felt no resentment against the stewards, but against Sleator. All that time I'd had to put up with Arthur Thomas and all the drama. Enduring all that pressure, keeping everything going smoothly and winning on all those horses— not for myself, but for Sleator. He himself puts it down to jealousy, but I still maintain that there would have been no complaints if the whole thing had been organised properly.

I felt more for England now than for Ireland. I had grown to like the people and their way of life. I determined to stick it out. Perhaps I would have made it but for the booze. I thought of that lovely little thatched house next door to the Saxon churchyard in Birlingham and all those splendid Rimell horses; of the great Fulke Walwyn and the sporting, rich Hugh Sumner. I'd turned all that down for a hero who had feet of clay. He'd let me down. Now there was nothing.

After the initial shock, terrible depression set in. Shirley and I had just finished doing up the garden of our new house. We had two lovely children, Caroline, who was now five years old, and Peter, who was four. They were happy at their nursery school. The future seemed assured. I was convinced that, given normal success, I would have been able to set up as a trainer in England, like my Uncle Rufus.

It was near the end of the season. Derek Ancil offered me the job of stable-jockey to his small string for the coming season. It was not very exciting, but I liked Derek and it meant that I was still in business.

Back in Ireland that summer, Willy O'Grady invited me to stay and ride for him. It was tempting and I was probably wrong not to accept. Although an alcoholic, he was an outstanding trainer and a delightful little man. But I turned him down because I wanted to continue riding in England. I didn't want to run away from that scene, from all my many friends, from my new way of life. I got on so well with all the trainers and was generally treated extremely well. I actually believed I was growing up.

However, when we returned to England, the depression started to creep in. Nothing much was happening now. The good days were over. My rides were few and far between. A lot of trainers, for whom, but for Sleator I could have ridden, now had other jockeys. I'd lost my contacts, my main job and, I discovered, my dedication too. Sleator had another jockey in Ireland riding my good horses. I was neither one thing nor the other. I was in limbo.

I used to go to the race-meetings, hoping for a spare ride and inevitably gravitate towards the bar. I threw myself heart and soul into the gas life with its night-clubs, booze and birds. My weight was getting tricky and I was nothing like as fit as I used to be. But there were still moments of fun with the lads.

My fellow Irish rider, Eddy Harty, a better horseman than jockey, could talk the hind leg off a donkey, and had an unusually high opinion of his own ability. One day, at Sandown, after a race which he had won, I found him sitting on a bench in the changing-room in floods of tears.

'What's the matter?' I asked.

'Go away,' he said. 'Can't you see I'm in a highly emotional state?'

'But you should be happy. You won, didn't you?'

'It's not that', he said, dissolving in tears again. 'I just can't get over how brilliant I was!'

But I went to the races less and less. As well as enjoying what the spivs in London were still prepared to give me, I found plenty of opportunity for living it up nearer home. I got more involved with a crowd of drinking types round Leamington, including a couple of Coventry City footballers. We would get together in a small club and start drinking in the morning. I was becoming dependent on alcohol. Perhaps I would have survived for quite a bit longer like that.

It was not to be. On November 11, I rode a three-year-old of Derek Ancil's, called Post Mark, in his first race over hurdles at Nottingham. He fell at the fourth hurdle and, as I lay there, half a dozen horses galloped over me. I was taken off to Nottingham General Hospital, where they found that I had lost all my remaining teeth, my gum on the lower jaw had been smashed and my bottom lip was split down to my chin. I had to have sixty stitches and I was such a sight that, when a friend, a real tough guy, came to see me, he ran out. He couldn't bear to look at my disfigured face. I thought the end of the world had come and I remember saying to a nurse the morning after the operation: 'It will stay like this for ever and ever. If you can find a gun, I'll shoot myself.' She said that in time it would go down and I might be all right. In fact, the plastic surgeon did a wonderful job, but it took a long time for the scars to go. Some of them are still visible.

I made a tremendous effort to get back on the racecourse again and got to Newbury just a fortnight later to ride Right Noble in a novice hurdle. We were second, beaten, ironically, by Willy Robinson on a horse of Fulke Walwyn's. It was in his very next race that Right Noble met his end at Sandown, as I recounted earlier.

When I arrived at Newbury, I had only just had the stitches removed and I was such a sight that a lot of people didn't recognise me. In fact, one trainer's wife suggested that I should retire, because I'd taken enough stick. To hell with it, I thought, I'll see it through. But I'd reckoned without two factors. First, a number of people thought I must have lost my nerve, and secondly the booze was taking over.

With so little riding now, I would find my way into that cellar bar at Cheltenham long before the last race. There everyone would be in great form. Bottles would be flying and Beasley would be the life and soul of the party. I'm getting hardened now, I thought. I can drink an awful lot without falling about. Why should I be the good all-Irish kid, when it doesn't matter any more? I've come a long way from those days in Ireland when I wouldn't be seen dead in a bar. I wander out to my old Zodiac, sitting all by itself in the trainers' and jockeys' car park. Like me, it's a loner. We travel alone now. I stop at a few places on the way home and I come back late for dinner. I don't eat it, because I know I'm slipping and I feel guilty. I'm disgusted with myself for falling so far from what I was when she married me and so I take it out on Shirley, imagining that she's annoyed with me for being late and pissed. I never hit her, but I catch hold of her by the shoulders and shake her. She never answers back and this makes me worse. I'm always ranting and raving.

She books my rides and is a tremendous help, always covering up for me. I have plenty of sex with her, but she has gone cold. So I rant all the more because she doesn't get turned on.

It's a double-edged sword now. I feel I am hurting her, and at the same time I'm starting to feel that she doesn't want me. I'm beginning to think there's something wrong with me, but I don't know what it is. I'm not getting the affection and help with this inner trouble that subconsciously I need and want. Shirley probably thinks I'm turning into a terrible bastard.

And, if she thought that, she was right. Sometimes, I'd slip off to London, on the pretext of riding at Kempton or Sandown, and stay the night in order to bask once more in the booze and beautiful bodies that the spivs were still prepared to provide. I used to make the excuse that I was staying with Monty Cosky, whom Shirley knew as an old friend of Arthur Thomas.

By now, in the knowledge that things were going badly for me, the punters and bookmakers were becoming bolder. I started receiving frequent telephone calls from men who suggested that, if we were to meet, we could organise some hot things and make ourselves a lot of money.

On the way back from Plumpton, where the station is so near the track that the last fence was burnt down by a cigarette thrown from a train, I found myself in a carriage full of men whom I had never seen before, but who called me Bobby. They were very friendly and filled me up with booze before making their well-planned proposition. If I would work for them, stopping well-backed horses or by ensuring that favourites ridden by other jockeys did not win, they would pay me the big money I so obviously needed. But even in my most alcoholic moments, I remembered my father's last words to me and although, God knows, I sank low, I was never low enough to go bent.

I was now riding anything that I was offered. At Warwick I was due to partner the outsider in a two-horse chase, trained, I think, by Roy Whiston, a very good chap and an excellent trainer. But this one was moderate and the favourite looked a certainty.

The day before the meeting a stranger telephoned, claiming that he knew me. If I didn't win, he said, he would make it worth my while. After the race the rendezvous would be the nearest Services to Leamington on the M1 motorway. I was to sit in the cafe and a man would give me an envelope containing £500 in readies. The same old fee, but now it was really big money, desperately needed. I told him that the best thing he could do was to back my horse and put the telephone down.

With half a mile to go in the race I was three fences behind. It would have been the easiest thing in the world to drop him out and collect that lovely 'monkey', but I persevered. The favourite broke down jumping the last fence and I just got up to win by a neck, earning myself the handsome sum of £13!

On top of the booze I was suffering from almost permanent concussion. I accepted a ride for a chicken farmer in a three-year-old hurdle at Southwell. He assured me that the animal had been well schooled. When it turned over with me at the first, he explained indignantly that, as he had no schooling hurdles, he had put a few bales of straw in his orchard and it had seemed to negotiate them all right.

Another man at Nottingham admitted that his horse hadn't jumped before, but that it was bred to jump. It fell! An even worse complication than the concussion came in the form of the piss-pills, which another jockey introduced me to at a party. Even though I was eating little—for four months after my Nottingham fall I couldn't chew and Shirley sieved all my food—the alcohol and inactivity sent my weight soaring. I discovered that, even after a night on the tiles, these pills would take off five or six pounds. Their effects were terrible. When I was riding, my hands would lock. I would get appalling cramp. Cantering down to the post, I would take my feet out of the stirrup-irons in an attempt to get the circulation back into my toes. I got wicked cramp, particularly in my thighs. And after the race I'd be blowing hard, shockingly distressed. I started on Saluric, then, finding that wasn't strong enough, switched to Hydra-saluric and finally to Lassix, the most potent of them all. I knew a chemist near home and had no trouble getting the pills on which I was soon relying.

Although nine months earlier my riding weight had been 10 st 5 lb, I had to take off 7 lb to do 11 st 3 lb, when Toby Balding asked me to ride Go Gailey in a three-mile hurdle at Kempton in February 1968. I won comfortably, but I was far from comfortable when I came in to unsaddle. It's only a few yards from the Kempton winners' enclosure to the weighing-room, but I could hardly see as I took off my saddle and it seemed like the longest walk. I weighed in, staggered into the changing-room and collapsed on a seat. Terry, who had long experience of the pills, rushed to get me a glass of half-neat salt and forced me to drink it. One doctor told me: 'If you don't give them up, you'll be dead in two years.' But I lived on them, increasing the dose to as many as three a day. I had to give up a number of rides because I was quite incapable on account of them. They counteracted the effects of the booze on my weight and I pepped myself up again with booze and dexedrine. But I still rode in frightful pain with red-hot pokers in my chest as I tried to breathe. They affected my hearing, too, and I got to the stage where I could tell how much I weighed by the ease with which my breeches went on, because my legs swelled up so much. I learnt later that they are designed for patients with high blood-pressure and drain the blood from the head and extremities.

One day coming back from the races, I was drunk and Shirley was driving, doing 70 m.p.h. on a straight road. I wanted to drive and she knew that I was in no fit state. I caught hold of the wheel and pulled violently towards a lay-by. We turned round twice in the road and just missed a car coming in the opposite direction. I don't know how she kept control. She was such a good driver. It was a miraculous escape.

Then we went to Josh Gifford's wedding, where there was all the champagne in the world. I had a wonderful day and was in a terrific state as I set off to drive home. In Banbury I drove around the cross six times, roaring and screaming. Up near the hospital on the Oxford road, Shirley decided she'd had enough. Scared stiff, she got out. As she was leaving the car, I drove on and she fell in the road. I reversed back and nearly ran her over. The rear wheel was actually on her coat.

Small wonder that our marriage was starting to suffer and that we were drifting further and further apart. Yet I loved her and needed her more than ever. I had always believed in the sanctity of marriage. But here in England it didn't seem to matter much. The girls were more flexible and the married ones seemed even easier than the single birds. All my ideas about marriage and religion were altering fast. I found that poor Shirley and I were not able to communicate any more. This frustrated me and I blamed her for not helping me.

I stopped bothering about going to the races, unless I was asked to ride. I would get up just in time to reach the off-licence where I'd buy a bottle of Martini or sherry (sometimes both), which I was hooked on at that time. Then I would go home and shut myself in a cupboard with the bottles and a record-player, swilling steadily as Herb Alpert's *Casino Royale* blared out incessantly and banging the wall in time to the music with a poker, which soon dug a deep hole. Sheer frustration. I was lost. I couldn't get through to anybody or anything.

Then, leaving the empty bottles, I'd go out at opening time to join my new friends, who regarded me as a real tough gas man. I felt that the good life was slipping away and, as the London gas was going, I lowered my standards steadily. I might stay in the club until the early hours, or I might pick up a different sort of bird during the day, the desperate married types who wanted sex more than company, and I wouldn't go home. There was a woman in Balsall Common . . . there were so many.

Then the next morning—I wouldn't drink any more. This was going to be a good day. I'd walk round the shops with no aim or object. I'd just buy half a bottle and take it home. But that was soon finished and I'd be off again to buy yet another half and then a whole one.

Our accountant told us we couldn't go on. I was badly in arrears with tax and mortgage. We must sell our house. I tried desperately to pull myself together and rode a few good races at courses like Doncaster and Ascot. And, when I won on Marcus Brutus at Lingfield for my old friend, Fred Winter, I felt that perhaps I was on the way back. I was even able to delight my Leamington friends by winning on the same horse at our local meeting, Warwick. But although racing is a small world and I was hitting the bottle, I told myself that I hadn't slipped too far, that I could soon be back on top again if only the chance would come.

It came.

CHAPTER 13

The Calm Before the Storm

Fred Winter had been training for four seasons. Just as he had been when a jockey, he was already right at the top of his profession with two Grand Nationals to his credit.

I had ridden only seven winners that season, when he sent for me and I drove down to meet him at Uplands, his red-brick Georgian house, nestling below Mann Down hill just outside the village of Lambourn in Berkshire.

Still the same Fred, kind and straight, he was now possessed of an even greater air of authority and personality. He was parting from his stable-jockey, Eddy Harty, and was interviewing me for one of the very best jobs in the business. I believe that Dave Dick had suggested me.

Relaxed and half-smiling as ever, he told me that, after my eighteen months in the wilderness, he was not quite sure about me. He had obviously heard the gossip that I was a very different man from the one he had so often ridden against. He asked me a series of pertinent questions and finally said: 'Right. You're on probation till Christmas. We'll see how you get on and how you behave yourself.'

Dick Francis, the former champion and Royal jockey, who

was fast becoming one of the world's leading writers of thrillers, wrote in the *Sunday Express*:

Bobby Beasley is to ride next season for Fred Winter, a match of champions if ever there was one. They are two of the only three post-war jockeys to have achieved the treble of Grand National, Cheltenham Gold Cup, and Champion Hurdle. The other is Willie Robinson.

Beasley won the National on Nicolaus Silver (1961), the Gold Cup on Roddy Owen (1959), and the Champion Hurdle on Another Flash (1960).

This was the period when Winter was at his peak riding horses like Sundew, Kilmore, Saffron Tartan, Mandarin, Clair Soleil, Fare Time and Eborneezer.

Few trainers can ever have been able to observe and judge their future jockeys at closer quarters than Winter did when riding against such a tough opponent as Beasley. Few trainers know so intimately the way their jockey's mind works. This alliance looks all set to be an harmonious and profitable one.

Most trainers expect miracles from their jockeys, and the better they were at riding themselves, the bigger the miracles they expect. They itch to be out there doing it.

Some have been seen to hop up and down in frustration. They greet their returning (defeated) jockey with a disgusted 'Why the hell didn't you . . . ?'

Having recovered during the season from terrible facial injuries sustained in a fall at Nottingham last November, 31-year-old Beasley has recently ridden six times for Fred—three firsts, two seconds, and one third.

On this showing when they get properly into their swing, punters regularly following them are in for a bonanza.

Beasley became available after fellow countryman Paddy Sleator was barred from sending Irish runners regularly to Arthur Thomas at Warwick, and has spent

most of a disjointed season riding at odd times for anyone
who asked.

This unsatisfactory situation at one time had Bobby
ready to pack up and head back across the Irish Sea. But
the new opportunity is bound to remind English racegoers
what a loss that would have been.

Fred Winter has parted on amicable terms from former
stable jockey Eddie Harty, who will continue to ride for
the stable when needed. Richard Pitman will continue on
the light weights, as Beasley's minimum is 10 st 12 lb.

Beasley's racing pedigree and record are formidable.
His grandfather won the 1891 Grand National on Come
Away, and his father's brother won it three times. His wife
Shirley's father, Arthur Thompson, won the National
twice (Sheila's Cottage and Teal).

His own father was champion jockey of Ireland for
several years. Bobby himself was Irish champion in 1960,
and runner-up to Stan Mellor in this country in 1961–62.

Quiet and very strong, Bobby Beasley is a beautiful
horseman with dynamite in his legs and velvet in his
hands. He shies away from limelight and is apt because
of that to be underrated. Fred's stable lives in the limelight.

Shirley was even more thrilled than I was. The misery that
she associated with Leamington was over. Her husband was
once again a top jockey. I tried to convince myself that I had
the drink sufficiently under control. So it was a very happy
little family that packed its bags and set out for Lambourn,
where so many of our friends, including Stan and Elain Mellor,
lived.

Fred had taken an ideal house for us. If you leave Lambourn
and drive north passing Uplands and Fulke Walwyn's lovely
cream-coloured Saxon House, you turn right off the main
Ashbury road and wind through the little hamlet of Upper
Lambourn, passing first the little house, which was Lester

Piggott's somewhat infrequent school and then the impressive red-brick Kingsdown establishment, where Peter Nelson trained the Derby winner Snow Knight. Thence a deserted road runs up a slight incline for more than a mile until it finally peters out on to the downs at an isolated farm called Maddle, where our little house was situated.

Lambourn itself is a very large village with a thriving industry, making the best motor horseboxes, and a number of shops, including an excellent chemist (which is also the local wine-merchant), a betting-shop and a large red-brick pub in the square—the Red Lion Hotel.

The lads exercise their horses in the morning and are apt to spend the afternoon until evening stables at about half past four, standing around the main street and outside the betting-shop. That popular trainer George Beeby once said it reminded him of a mining village on strike.

If I had known Lambourn better and had realised what was actually wrong with me, I would have avoided it like the plague, because all the parties held there throughout the year made it a lethal place for a heavy drinker. But I told myself that this was my last chance and, as we settled into our quiet little house, I think I even persuaded myself that I would be able to keep off the booze.

The new life started well. It was great to be getting up early every morning to drive to Uplands, ride out with Fred's string of decent horses, getting to know them as I galloped and schooled them up on Mann Down as the summer drew to a close. Our first runners at the early meetings showed distinct promise and on September 21 we had our first winner, Soloning, at Taunton.

By the beginning of October, Bob Butchers of the *Daily Mirror*, under the headline 'Beasley on top again', wrote:

Decision of Fred Winter to engage Bobby Beasley to ride for him this season is putting the Irish jockey right back among the winners where he belongs.

Beasley, who rode his 300th English winner earlier this month, seriously considered returning to Ireland or emigrating after riding only seven winners here last season. Admittedly, he was hindered by a couple of bad falls, but far too often he was on the stands watching less capable jockeys in action.

Bobby's five wins this season have all been for Winter . . .

Fred is usually a slow starter, trying to time most of his horses for the big races in the second half of the season, but in the next few weeks I had ridden quite a few more, including two on Lord Howard de Walden's Athenaeum, a double at Windsor and three in two days at Newbury. I was still drinking more than was really good for me, but regular work, plenty of physical exercise and the need to keep fit was holding it at bay. It looked as though Shirley and I would make a go of it again.

Then, at Newbury on November 29, fate struck again. The novice chaser Latour, one of my earlier winners, fell at the fifth fence. I broke my wrist and was out of action again. I have seldom been sorry for myself, but I was on this occasion. It was a cruel blow and, although I would have done so sooner or later, I went straight back on the booze to seek consolation. Christmas was coming and I was only too ready to join the celebrations.

Christmas Day was one of the worst ever. I went to a party in the morning and didn't get back until about half past two, by which time I was plastered, the dinner was ruined and Shirley and the children were extremely upset.

As the wrist mended, I started to ride out again, but now, instead of hope, there was this strange feeling of frustration, which I'd had in Leamington when I made the hole in the wall. I wanted Shirley, her love and affection more than ever, but at the same time I knew I was driving her away and creating an unbridgeable gap between us.

I was drinking heavily and was starting to lose my self-respect. I felt that my career was over and that I hadn't very long to ride. So what the hell did anything matter? The dedication had gone. More and more I was driving down to the chemists for bottles, bringing them home and drinking surreptitiously, hiding the empties in a shed until I found the opportunity to bury them in a hole in the ground. I was parading my boozing publicly. I gravitated to the pubs, where the boozy types of stable-lads met—the Red Lion and the Malt Shovel, which was just next door to our yard. I gate-crashed a lads' party in a canteen at Lambourn, drove across a lawn and into a tree.

This tough gas man started to ride out in dark glasses, revelling in my hangover, inviting the kind of ribald comments that are made about famous 'lushes'. Sometimes the eyes behind the glasses were bloodshot, sometimes black, because Shirley was now using a vicious left hook in an attempt to control me. The lads thought this was very funny. One day for no reason I threw a knife at her. Thank God, it just missed, but only just. It stuck in the wood half an inch behind her head.

The parties got fewer. There has always been plenty of drunkenness around Lambourn, but I was going too far. I was bad news. I would stagger out of bed in the morning and peer round the curtains at the car in the drive to see if there were any dents, or worse still, blood on its wings. Several times I met people in the village, who told me: 'God, you weren't half swinging last night', and I asked what I had done. 'Bloody hell!' they said, 'you went spare'. 'Where was I?' 'You were at so-and-so's and you were doing this and you raped that one.' 'Who was it I raped?' I couldn't even remember that. 'Did I insult anybody?' 'Oh, yes, you told somebody that he was "a right fucker"!' So for the rest of that day, I would drive off in my car for fear of meeting someone whom I had unknowingly insulted. These blackouts were terrifying. I could have murdered somebody without even knowing it.

The people in the farmhouse at Maddle were very good friends, who realised the state I was in, and tried to help me. I used to go roaring in and out in my car like a demented demon; they built a sort of humped back obstacle across the drive to slow me down or I'd have killed their young children.

I often have nightmares about those days when I drove round the area like a madman, forcing others off the road because I was driving on the wrong side.

One night Shirley and I were invited out to dinner with Fulke and Cath Walwyn. Delightful people, full of fun, loved and immensely respected by all, they now deservedly train for the Queen Mother. I was well away before we arrived at Saxon House and made a frightful exhibition of myself, monopolising the conversation, carrying on about sex and contraception. I ranted on about Irish girls being frigid. Actually I didn't know whether they were or not, because I'd never been with any of them. Of course I was really attacking Shirley and all Roman Catholic girls, unconcerned that my hostess was also a Catholic. No wonder we were no longer asked out by decent people. I now know that my rude, insulting behaviour is a symptom of alcoholism. It's a Jekyll and Hyde condition. Most alcoholics are not rude when they're sober and frequently cannot remember insulting others when they're drunk. Inevitably out of shame they come to resist the decent folk and slide steadily down to drinking in a society, where they think they are appreciated, even admired.

I had my first ride in public again at Kempton on January 31. It fell. Those two months since Latour's fall at Newbury had done a lot of damage. Fred was marvellous, trying to pick and choose my mounts and I won a race on March 8 with Sparrow Hawk at Haydock. Fred put me on quite a few more winners right through to the end of the season. There was a nice double at Windsor. But at another Windsor meeting, I rode three well-fancied horses and they all ran shockingly. I'd had a good few drinks on the way and I was terrible. My reflexes had gone and, when the time came to pick a horse up,

The Napton Handicap Chase, Warwick, February 1964.
Gaymoss (ridden by myself), on the left, is coming
up to beat Double Cross II (ridden by Stan Mellor). *(Bernard Parkin)*

This is me—dislodged from Chevenne at the last fence
in the Compton Handicap Chase at Wolverhampton, 1965. *(Sport & General)*

Above left: My brother and my mother—
a beautiful woman like her sister, Valerie Hobson.

Above right: Peter, Shirley and myself.
Dark glasses for a real hard man with a hangover!

Below: Father Christmas is not at his best—
with Peter, Caroline and Shirley after the Nottingham fall.

Above left: My aunt, Mrs John Profumo (Valerie Hobson). *(Sport & General)*
Above right: Helping the Mayor at a Warwick charity show for spastic children.
Below: Summer 1967: another charity show for spastic children.
Left to right: Jackie (Tesco) Cohen, Bob Butler, Johnny Buckingham (now a
jockey's valet) on his 100 to 1 National winner, Foinavon, and myself in the
striped shirt showing my debauchery all too clearly.

The actual Second Start: on Norwegian Flag after winning at Leopardstown in 1971. They retrieved my cap in time to be led in! *(Ruth Rogers)*

On Captain Christy over the last fence to win the P.Z. Chase at Thurles.
'We won all right. He was a brilliant devil, but you had to sit
tight when he hit a fence as he had this one.' *(Ruth Rogers)*

Above: A champion in action!
The comeback—winning on Captain Christy at Punchestown.

Below: On Captain Christy after the final triumph, 1974. *(Rex Coleman)*

nothing was happening. It was like a car with a slipping clutch. There was no drive. I just went through the motions. Occasionally a bit of the old inspiration returned momentarily. I rode a fair race to finish fifth to Persian War on Into View in the Champion Hurdle and I actually won the valuable Heinz Chase at Ascot with Beau Champ on April 12. All these were for Fred. Scarcely any other trainer offered me a ride. I had let down friends like Toby Balding. I was letting down Fred. I wouldn't have blamed him had he believed that I was deliberately stopping some of his fancied horses. The old telephone calls had started again and I certainly could have done so to make myself some readies, but I didn't. Even in my fuddled mind, I knew that I owed Fred more than I had ever owed Sleator. He alone was giving me a chance to come back and I would never have done anything to hurt him, even had I felt so inclined. The trouble was that usually, when it came to the crunch, there was just nothing there.

On my bad days, I always thought it was Shirley's fault for not loving me and for widening the gulf between us. This craving for affection is another well-known symptom. She was obviously disgusted with me—and who could blame her?

One evening at home, when the children were in bed, Shirley and I were sitting in complete silence on either side of the fireplace. Suddenly I jumped up and shouted: 'If you don't want to talk, fair enough. I'll go somewhere where I know somebody who will talk to me.'

I stormed out of the house, nearly broke the springs of the car on the hump, hurtled off to one of my pubs, where I ordered drinks all round and two large brandies for myself, and immediately, as though it had been fated, found what I was seeking. There in the bar, drinking her share, was a big, well-built redhead called Joyce. I'd seen her around and had thought that she was a fair bit of stuff. Now, as I started chatting to her, she was more than friendly. Our eyes met over our glasses and we clicked. At that moment, boozed and disenchanted with the sterility, the nothingness of home, I was ready to click with anybody. It just happened to be Joyce. She knew all about horses and racing and she looked game. So I decided to have a go.

That night I got very pissed. I can't remember where we went, but I know I made a fool of myself in front of everyone, as we danced around, kissing and fondling and falling about on top of each other. All the locals were laughing and I knew that Fred would get to hear about it. But I didn't care. The job and the race-riding could go to hell. I had found someone who was prepared to love me, smother me with the affection I was missing at home and to have fun with me.

I had reached a well-known alcoholic stage, where the dread of loneliness seized me. My world and my marriage had come to an end and I was grabbing. I was desperate for love and Joyce gave it to me with interest.

The affair blossomed. We went everywhere together. She even drove me to the races.

Fred had a word with me. He still didn't know my problem any more than I did. He just thought I was drinking too much. He told me quietly that he would rather I didn't mix in the village and didn't drink there. I was letting down the standard of the stable as well as myself. If I wanted to drink, then I should do it at home. I recognised the fairness of the rebuke, but took no notice. I had to have the drink, the company and the girl.

Joyce and I talked about going off together. Anywhere. I couldn't care less. I had visions of living in a flat and getting any job—washing dishes, even. I just wanted to run away. I was bordering on the insane. It had all been too much—the obsession for drink and women.

Some of the old Beasley was still left, but now it had turned to self-hatred and a hatred of riding and even of racing, the game I loved so much that once I had sold my soul to it.

In a moment of clarity, I had been to see a doctor. But he was no help. In common with many of his profession he just thought I was a weak-willed ne'er-do-well, who was drinking too much. If I pulled myself together, I could stop all this nonsense.

One day Shirley and I had an appalling row about Joyce, the drink and everything. In desperation she went to Fred to get help for herself. She was at her wits' end. She knew there was something wrong with me, but I was quite uncontrollable. As we were living out of the way up at Maddle, most people, although they knew we didn't get on together, had blamed Shirley, believing that she was a bad-tempered, nagging woman, who treated me badly. It was, of course, the other way round.

The major part of Fred Winter's success is due to his superior intelligence and understanding of human and equine nature. Now, although he had no experience of alcoholism, a light dawned. He came up to Maddle and told me that all this time he had not known the true nature of my problem. He had just thought that I was drinking too much. Suddenly it had hit him. 'Bobby,' he said, 'you are a very, very sick man. You are an alcoholic. Go into hospital for treatment. It's coming towards the end of the season. Get yourself cured. Come back after the summer and your job will be waiting for you. You'll still be my stable-jockey. You can wash out all that has happened in the past and start afresh. Everything will be OK, I promise you.'

It's my greatest regret that I didn't take his advice then and there, because he would have stuck by me. He is so tolerant, kind, good and loyal. He could so easily have said: 'Clear off back to Ireland. Get out of the way!' But Fred's not like that. He's a pretty wonderful man.

I didn't want to know. I told him to go away and that I'd be all right. I'd manage. I wasn't an alcoholic. I just drank too much. I hadn't yet reached the rock bottom.

A little later, boozed to the eyebrows and still obsessed with Joyce, I had a terrible row with Shirley, threw all her baggage out and told her to 'Get out of my house. Fuck off. Get out of my fucking life!'

She did. She left in her own car and sent the children to Ireland with a friend.

When I sobered up the next day, I thought Christ, what have I done? I walked round the empty house in floods of tears, going in and out of the children's rooms. I was so desperate, that I set out to find her. Hysterically crazed, I drove round to all the places where I thought she might be. I knew that in her present condition, she wouldn't return to me. I was still going to Joyce for my physical love and affection, but at the same time I had to have Shirley and our children.

Eventually I found her, staying with some friends near Cirencester. They wouldn't let me in. They said that Shirley was on the verge of a breakdown, that she was under sedation and in no fit state to see anyone, least of all me. Then they slammed the door in my face.

I drove home and paced up and down all night. Everything I valued in life had gone. One of Fred's men came up to redecorate the house. I ranted and screamed at the poor fellow so that he beat a hasty retreat.

I didn't want Joyce, but I had to have her. The old cliche—she understood me and my wife didn't. All the same I never let her settle in at Maddle.

The next day I went back to see Shirley, but she had moved on. It took me a little while to discover that the Mellors had taken her in. I kept going to see her, but she wouldn't have anything to do with me and eventually she went back to stay with her parents and the children in Ireland. I was all alone at Maddle for the summer.

One day some friends of Joyce's who lived in Newbury telephoned. I apparently sounded very peculiar when I answered and, before we had finished talking, I had passed out. They were scared and drove sixteen miles out to Maddle to find me unconscious on the floor. They brought me round and took me home, giving Joyce and me their own room for a week. After a while I started to forget what had happened and, as I recovered, I kept telling Joyce that we must go away together. In the back of my mind I knew it would never happen, but she, poor girl, believed me. If I hadn't become such a bastard and had known what I was doing, I would have realised that I was using her as an emotional prop. I was very fond of her as a person and she was so good to me when I was in an appalling state. But I greatly regret treating her like this. We have since met and find we have little in common now. Fortunately she bears no resentment.

I returned to Maddle and, after many telephone calls to Ireland, Shirley came back to collect her belongings. She was accompanied by solicitors. In a stupid attempt to shock her into staying I suggested we should start divorce proceedings. The only effect it had was to send her to her own solicitors in Cardiff.

As she sorted out her clothes, I put my arm around her shoulders and said: 'Couldn't we talk about this?' She recoiled. 'You're not supposed to touch me,' she said. 'The lawyers said no contact.' When once more I tried to be affectionate she said: 'If you don't stop, these men are empowered to restrain you.' So she left and I went back to the bottle and Joyce.

The next four weeks were spent in a complete haze. Shirley has since filled in the gap. Apparently I found my way back to Ireland and stayed with Tom Conroy, a friend who lived down the road from Shirley's parents. She used to come and chat me to me. Apparently I even stayed in a hotel in Arklow and was drinking a great deal. I told her I was returning to England to arrange with Fred Winter about next year's riding.

Anyway, I went back to Maddle, and on May 7 I rode Rimmon to win a novice hurdle at Fontwell for Fred. I remember that all right because I had the devil of a job to get my weight down to 11 st 7 lb. I managed it somehow, although the deyhydrating piss-pills were no longer working properly and I had begun to retain fluid. But they still had their side-effects. It was the most horrible ride I've ever had. Constant pain through the race. Then I half collapsed as I dismounted and my hands locked as I tried to undo my girth straps. I knew this was the end of the road and that I had to retire. It took me two hours to recover and I don't know how I got into my car. On that terrible journey back to Lambourn I decided to telephone Shirley and tell her my decision. She was the only person I wanted to talk to. So we must have seen a lot of each other on my visit to Ireland. But she was out and I was told she would be staying in Ireland to look after her mother, who wasn't well.

God, I was lonely. If only there had been somebody to assure me I could keep riding I might have been all right. At least one of the great things about Alcoholics Anonymous, is that there's always somebody to ring up and talk to.

The next morning I went down to Fred and told him my decision. I explained how very good he'd been to stand by me, but I didn't want to let him down any more. Even if I went to hospital and got treatment, it would be too late to start again and ensure getting through next season. Obviously my trip to Ireland had done some good and gave me the hope of keeping my family united, if nothing else.

I poured out my feelings of remorse and guilt for everything that I had done to Fred, my wife and family, my friends in Lambourn, the job and myself. Fred talked to me again for a long time, trying to reassure me that he would stand by me and it didn't matter what people thought. But all his goodwill and understanding were in vain. Like a typical alcoholic, I'd reached the point of no return. My mind had gone. Mentally I was in no position to stand and fight, because the sense of guilt is too great. I could take no more. So, when he offered me the ride on a certainty in a chase, saying: 'She only has to canter round. It'll be a nice way to go out', I was very grateful, but I said I couldn't do it. I chose another horse for my last ride. It ran a bad third. The mare won easily. I had set out to destroy myself and I had succeeded.

As I waited in Lambourn for the furniture removers to

come and take our things back to Ireland, Fred suggested that I might as well ride out to pass the time. They put me on a sturdy raw young horse, who had only recently been broken and I told the Guv'nor: 'I really believe this is a racehorse.' It was the one the lads called 'the cob', the future champion hurdler and chaser, Bula.

After riding out, I would drink until the pubs closed and then go to the chemist and collect two bottles of Cyprus sherry. With them I would drive up to the top of the famous White Horse Hill and sit by myself on those wonderful virgin downland gallops, swilling my drink and gazing out over the historic Vale of the White Horse, towards my beloved Cheltenham that I would never see again. Then, drunk with cheap wine and self-pity, I would drive back to more booze and Joyce's loving arms. It was a long, hot summer.

The start of the new season was purgatory for me, thinking of what might have been. I even took out a licence again and had a couple of spare rides. But there was nothing. It had all gone.

So had my spending money. I had saved all my presents from Fred's owners and had a hoard of £1,100 in lovely crisp tenners. Now in two months it had all gone on so-called gas and booze.

The Press wrote up my retirement and one paper published a piece headed 'BOBBY BEASLEY TO CALL IT A DAY'. The next morning I received a letter from a London firm, asking whether I would be interested in a job selling insurance. I went for an interview with the managing director, who told me that they were looking for former sports stars with contacts. For some obtuse alcoholic reason, I accepted and agreed to start a crash course in about a month's time at Carshalton in Surrey.

Finally the removers arrived at Maddle with their containers and, with one or two exceptions, everyone in the Lambourn area said a heartily relieved goodbye to Bobby Beasley.

CHAPTER 14

Rock Bottom

On my way home I wondered why I'd taken this extraordinary job at £20 a week among people whom I didn't know. The answer was that I wanted to punish myself for the scandal over Joyce and all the degradation I'd inflicted on Shirley. I consoled myself with the knowledge that the children were still too young to register. I thought it was a chance to run away from the village where I had earned so much shame and I thought that, as I would still be in contact with racing people, perhaps I could make a success of it and restore some of my self-respect.

I didn't know what I was going to do when I got home to Enniscorthy. I couldn't live with my in-laws, who would take a long time to forgive me for the terrible things I had done to their daughter. And the farm, which I had bought in 1961, had not yet been properly renovated. The builders were just starting to do up the house.

First I spent a week in a hotel and, finding it too expensive, stayed with my farmer friend Tom Conroy again. After a while, I moved into my empty farmhouse, caring nothing for the fact that it was in a complete shambles and had no glass in the windows. I slept on a mattress on the floor like a hippie, and grew a beard. As I'd become a bum I might as well behave like one. I'd shock these bloody Irish bastards. Subconsciously I was blaming Ireland bitterly for throwing me into an environment I couldn't handle. This was all mixed up alcoholic thinking.

However, although the beard grew red and grey and I went around in the scruffiest clothes I could find, Shirley and I seemed to come together again. She went to Mass every Sunday. I even went with her and the children a few times. Then one day I went to confession. I said to the priest that the doctor had told Shirley it would be dangerous with her toxaemia to have another child. She might easily die. I didn't trust or go in for the 'safe period', but I was a normal man. Surely in the circumstances, it would be right to use contraceptives?

Through the grille came that awful disembodied voice loud and clear: 'Carry on normally. It's a sin to use contraception. If she conceives and dies, it's the will of God.'

I got up off my knees and told him exactly what he could do with his hypocritical Roman Catholic Church and stomped out. I've never been back. I was finished for good with the Catholic Church in Ireland. This doesn't mean that I don't believe in God. I do, wholeheartedly. The product is all right, but the salesmen are rotten. The awful thing is that they are now talking about changing the rules. What will happen then? Will all those people who have suffered be transformed from Hell to Heaven?

Yes, beard and booze and all, I had got closer to Shirley again, so that she did indeed conceive and, in the fullness of time, our third child, Helen, was to be born safely, which in no way condoned the priest's iniquitous ruling. God knows why, after the way I had treated her, but Shirley had been missing me. In the quiet of her parents' home, in the Irish atmosphere, where we had met, married and had so much fun, she had had time to think and to realise that perhaps there was a glimmer of a chance that we might save our marriage and the family. Moreover, freed from the pressures of Lambourn and, particularly, from the piss-pills, I was loving and persuasive.

One other point. Whereas in England a paralytic drunkard is looked on with disgust, in Ireland he (or she) is accepted as a normal part of the scene just as a man who doesn't drink is looked on as an abnormal sissy. I was among old friends who thought none the worse of me and enjoyed some gas drinking.

So I had no wish to return to England for the insurance people, who were now writing me urgent letters. I don't know to this day what made me go through with the thing. My mind was quite deranged, but I somehow thought that I couldn't just wait around for the house to be renovated and extended. I must be doing something. Amidst all the mad turmoil in my fuddled brain, there was still a need to prove myself again and in some way to make a fresh start. But I was afraid to leap into the unknown and there was always the fact that I didn't need to go. We still had just enough money in Ireland to rub along until the house was completed.

So I shaved off my beard, packed my bags and drove off in my little Fiat to the docks. The car was loaded and lowered into the hold of the boat. I went to the bar and started drinking. I was terrified and, as I got drunker, I felt an irresistible longing for Shirley and home. I went down to the hold and told the men that I'd had an urgent telegram from home, saying that my mother was ill. I must go back home at once. Could they let me have my car back? Complaining that they'd never done such a thing before, they very reluctantly unloaded the car and I drove to Wexford for a few more weeks.

A second time I summoned up courage and actually crossed the Irish Channel. I drove as far as Haverfordwest, turned round, back to the boat and home again. I did it a third time and got as far as Cardiff before I was gripped by the fear of loneliness and went all the way back to Wexford. At the fourth try I made it. But I discovered that I only knew the English racecourses. So I drove to Kempton, where I had arranged to meet my brother, who would guide me to Purley. But when I got to the deserted Sunbury track, he wasn't there. I couldn't really blame him because the last time we'd met I had broken his finger in one of my violent blackouts.

I waited two hours and then drove the only way I knew back to Lambourn, where I stayed for a few days with Fred Winter's assistant, Peter Tabor. There I contacted my brother and asked him to arrange digs for me in the Purley area. On the way to London, I called in at Ascot sales with Fred and watched him buy his future crack chaser, Pendil. God, what a state I must have been in! I telephoned my brother, who had not been able to find digs. So I made my way to London and stayed with my old friend, Jimmy the Spiv, with whom I sampled some of the old London gas, and finally reported to the managing director of the company.

There were a number of potential insurance salesmen on the week's crash course. After we were passed out and posted to our areas, our salaries would soon stop and we would be on commission. So I acted like an idiot, pretended not to understand and spun it out so that I took the course three times.

The man who turned out best was a Yorkshire coal-miner, who didn't understand it at all, but had a great way of talking. I hated it. My mind—such as was left of it—was only half on it. The pull of racing was always there. I watched the papers to see how horses that I should have been riding were performing. Then I thought of Shirley, pregnant in Ireland and I felt so lonely.

One weekend I drove down to Portsmouth to see my mother and went out drinking with one of our relatives. We got into a bierkeller full of sailors and very strong lager. I put back enough to sink a battleship and blacked out, although outwardly I appeared all right. This is common in alcoholics. Only Shirley, who knew me so well, could tell when I was in a blackout by the glazed expression in my eyes. My uncle had no way of knowing until he got into the car beside me. He told me afterwards that I drove right through a closed market, knocking over stalls. There were oranges and potatoes flying, men cursing and people diving out of the way. Then I careered on right to the top of a multi-storey car-park and back down again the wrong way. It was very lucky that nobody was hurt. I was almost insane.

I had opted to sell my insurance in Leamington, the only area, apart from Lambourn, that I knew well. I found myself thrown into a situation I had never had to cope with. My life had always been organised. Even in Lambourn at the end, I'd still had a home to go to. Now for the first time I was alone in digs, drying my socks in front of the fire, looking for coins for the meter to keep me from dying of cold, eating in transport cafes to save money.

In any case, I ate very little because I needed all I had for booze. A few jockeys bought insurance policies from me out of kindness, but otherwise I couldn't summon up courage to knock on people's doors and tell them the tale. A former professional footballer, a big handsome chap, was supposed to be initiating me into the job. He took me round with him sometimes to show me how he did it. One day he said: 'I'm expected at this place.' He rang the door-bell and it was opened by a smashing blonde, obviously wearing nothing under her housecoat. When she saw me, she was annoyed and said to my friend: 'I didn't think you'd have anyone with you. Go away and come back on your own!'

The little money I had was in Ireland. Now the depression set in again and I sank to a lower level than ever. The snow came late that winter, at the end of February and the beginning of March. One morning when I left my digs, I slopped through the dirty slush on the pavements, feeling my feet growing soaking wet because my shoes had holes in them. I was waiting around for opening time when I saw a grand pair of shoes in a shop window, went away and returned. I looked down at my own sodden feet. Then I thought no, if I buy those shoes, I won't have enough for the booze.

My grandmother had left me a portable TV set. It was my

only bit of luxury. But the need for booze was getting worse and, as I say, I wasn't eating because it interfered with my drinking. I *had* to have that alcohol. So I sold my TV set for a tenner.

My favourite haunt in Leamington was Sid's Bar, where the barman, a big Galway fellow called Joe Keane, was a great friend and help. He'd known me from the old days. Every day he gave me soup and held out hope. He was always trying to get me back to Ireland, but by now I felt too ashamed to return. On the morning before Bula won the Gloucester Hurdle at Cheltenham's National Hunt Festival, I was sitting, as usual, slumped over Joe's old counter, a debauched thirteen stone, and he said: 'I bet you one day you'll be riding at Cheltenham again.'

The next afternoon I sat in a sleazy little room in my digs with an old bird, who had a TV set, and cried to myself, as I watched Soloning win the Arkle Challenge Trophy, ridden by Paul Kellaway. Bula and Soloning. Both trained by Fred. Both my rides.

At night I had wicked, terrible nightmares. I would wake with my heart pounding and a desperate pain in my head as though it was going to explode. In the morning—frightful remorse. I'm not going to drink anymore, I told myself. Then, after a few drinks, I'm damned if I'm going to try to stop. More remorse. I'm the greatest bastard in the world. It's got me. Everyone's against me because I'm the worst bastard, but it's got me. I was mad. Later, I learnt that 95 per cent of people who reach this stage are in hospital under sedation, receiving proper treatment. I should have been committed. I was in the depths of despair, and needed help. But when people tried to help me, I wouldn't take it.

I was approached to sell 'hot' saddles. Worse, someone came into the bar and said he wanted a driver, who was willing to earn £500. Luckily Joe and I smelt a rat and in any case I was in no fit state. It turned out that they wanted the driver for the getaway car in a big armed robbery!

The insurance job was getting nowhere at all. I'd run out of jockeys. And the Company ran out of patience. My footballer-friend said I'd been given an ultimatum. If I couldn't earn a proper commission by selling a policy within a week, I was out. No more retaining salary. Fired. He said he had set one up for me, a nice couple who were all ready to buy and all I had to do was to go and sell. So I put on my smart suit, polished my shoes, took my briefcase and started off. Unfortunately, I badly needed some Dutch courage and stopped on the way for three large 'snorts', or 'squirts', as we call them in Ireland. I arrived, knocked on the door, was ushered into the front room, opened up my briefcase and, to a very receptive audience, started my little speech as I had been taught. They were certainly very nice people. And suddenly there came a momentary flash of the old Beasley. I crammed my papers back into the briefcase, stopped talking in mid-speech, stood up and said: 'Fuck it! This bloody policy's no good to you,' and ran out of the house.

Result, the sack. I stayed on in Leamington for a few more weeks, drifting, just mooching about, full of mad schemes. I even looked at a place where I could start training—some hope, with no money! I kept on the digs because I had saved a few bob in the bank as a last resort. I had told Shirley I was coming back, but I was now in such a state that I was even afraid to face my Irish friends. Sid's Bar was my constant refuge. One lunch time a smart businessman came in and whispered to Joe: 'Who's your friend in the cheap anorak?' I lived in the thing. I've kept it as a souvenir and wear it to milk the cows.

Then Fate again took a hand. By some incredible chance, I met a wonderful woman.

She was in her late thirties, smart, most attractive, highly intelligent and rich. I shall never know what she saw in me, a down-at-heel, desperate, suicidal, drunken bum. But there was an immediate mutual attraction, mental and physical. Although she had her own thriving businesses, she, too, was lost and lonely. Her marriage had broken up and she was temporarily floundering. Without being in any way sloppy, we were able to find solace in each other. We used to talk for hours into the night. I believe our meeting was arranged for both of us by God. We satisfied and soothed each other, and gave each other hope.

She never censured me for my drinking. In fact, we drank happily together. Joe's words had ignited a faint spark of hope, which she now fanned.

At the time I met her I was at rock bottom—completely finished. I had thoughts of drifting up to London or working on a building site. We became very fond of each other. And indeed out of my tremendous respect for her, I began to see the possibility of regaining my own self-respect. Even though she very much wanted me to stay for ever and said she would set me up in business with her, she persuaded me that first I must go back to Ireland, face any music there was to be faced, and see whether I couldn't get started again.

It was the most beautiful interlude of my life and I am happy to say that she knows just how much she did for me. She, too, has found contentment in re-marriage. Without her faith and her push, I would never have gone home.

When I arrived back at Enniscorthy in early summer, Shirley was about to have her baby. On top of that she had her own problems. The farm was still not finished, so once again I had to stay with Tom Conroy up the road.

I was still drinking as heavily as ever, but in my heart I knew now that I was suffering from the disease. I wouldn't admit it even to myself, but there was no doubt I was an alcoholic.

A few days after my return—again almost as though it had been ordained—my old friend Nicky Rackard and I realised that he was in the same state as myself. A fine big man, a great all-round athlete, he had been an Irish hurling champion and, with his first-class brain, had qualified and become the leading vet in Wexford. Then he had a set-back, got into trouble and lost his practice. His life was in ruins. He woke me up at half past five in the morning, said he'd been out all night picking mushrooms and asked me for a drink. We soon got through the bottle, which I always kept by my bed to start the day right. Nicky said: 'Let's go out for a few squirts.' And I saw that we were as bad as each other.

We got the pub open at half past eight and for two days we weren't seen. Neither of us can remember anything. They were lost days. When we partly sobered up, we felt terrible and decided to go to a barbecue at a friend's house. We were desperate cases. Half-way through the night Nicky, stoned out of his mind, stood on the bank of the Slaney River, which is wide and fast here, as it runs into the sea, and swore that he would swim across. Somehow I managed to save him from certain death. A few days went by before he telephoned again in the middle of the night. He was at least three-parts cut and he begged me to come and see him as soon as possible. I wasn't much better myself, but I went and found him terribly depressed and surrounded by empty bottles. He looked like death and indeed this was what he intended to seek. He blurted out that he could see no reason for going on, life was worthless and the time had come to finish it. What a sight we must have been; two hopeless drunks sloshing whisky into our glasses or drinking out of the bottle to save time. But suddenly I knew he meant what he said and the knowledge lent me courage and strength of purpose.

I became very angry, seized him by the shoulders and shouted: 'What in God's name do you think you're talking about, man? Look at me. I've lost my job and my marriage is in ruins. I've blown the lot and I have no education to fall back on, unlike a professional man, who can always go back when he's been cured. You're a qualified vet. You can go back to it any time you like. Just because you need drying out now doesn't mean you can't go back to vetting later. Because you know you can. Everybody knows you and you have lots of friends who trust you. Just take a look at me. Think what I've been through. How much have I to go back to?'

Somehow I managed to get through to him and the very

next day he went into hospital and thence to Alcoholics Anonymous. It had a profound effect on me, but I still obstinately believed I was different and could carry on. Beasley was no sodden lush like Rackard. Wasn't he the hard man, who just drank too much?

But forces were at work. Shirley had her baby daughter, Helen, and I received a call from Stuart Barratt, who had seven horses. He wanted me to help him train them on the sands at Portmarnock. I went to see him and agreed to help, but I refused point blank to ride them. There was a mental block. I just would not get on a horse's back.

Stuart was gloriously mad, full of wild, eccentric ideas. Nobody else really knew how to train horses. He had decided that, instead of galloping, they should swim long distances. He planned to build a large raft to take them out to sea and then let them over the side to swim ashore. In the meantime, I was to do my best to make them swim and was provided with a frogman's outfit for the purpose. I'm told that Beasley, wet suit, flippers, goggles and all going down the streets to the strand followed by horses, was one of the sights of Wexford. Only two of the animals would go out far enough to swim. This was a fairly high proportion because most horses will only swim naturally when they can see the opposite bank. But we got two in and there were stories of the Loch Ness monster being sighted off Portmarnock!

Eventually I convinced Stuart that, as all the horses couldn't be exercised in this way, it would be better, at least for the time being, to train them all in the more orthodox way. He reluctantly agreed and I got them fairly fit, working them on the sands.

I stayed in the house with the Barratts, who had a large Afghan hound. One night they dressed up and went out to a party, leaving me on my own with a new bottle of gin. I was lonely and depressed. As I got half way through the bottle, I started dancing round with the dog on its hind legs, imagining that it was a woman and that I, too, was having a party. I

8—SS * *

finished the bottle. When they arrived home, they found me lying out cold on the floor with the dog in my arms.

They engaged a groom to help me. It turned out that he was a fanatic Maoist. To begin with I got on well with him as long as he thought I was an ordinary worker like himself and was prepared to be harangued constantly with the thoughts of Chairman Mao and of James Connolly.

The trouble started when he realised I was actually training the horses and he identified me as the boss's man. Now he would shout at me that I was a bourgeois tool of a capitalist pig. 'The days of the capitalist dogs are over! Mao says that when the tree is cut down, the capitalist monkeys will fall from it!'

One day when I was feeding the horses, he put on a pair of string riding gloves and suddenly hit me hard, unawares. Then sparring around me, he shouted: 'Come on and fight you capitalist bourgeois pig. You've no chance. I was an amateur champion.'

Now Beasley is no sort of boxing champion at all, but I was half-pissed and in any case didn't like being belted. I was wearing slippery suede shoes. So I said: 'Hold on a minute while I put my teeth in the car and take off my shoes.' I came back in my bare feet and took one swipe at him. It was a tremendous crack, which landed fair and square and split his eye open. He got on his bicycle and fled, never to be seen again.

Hearing the noise of the fight, Stuart came out with his gun, and we all went off and told the local Irish police, the Garda, that there was a mad Maoist loose. The senior chap scratched his head and asked: 'What sort of animal would that be?'

When I had been there about a month, we had a runner at Navan. Something stirred in me and, in the car on the way back, I said: 'I'll start riding on Monday.' I did and it just seemed as though I'd stopped only the day before. The barrier had gone. I rode a canter on the strand and felt great. Then we got a couple of jockeys over and I rode work with them. One said in surprise: 'My God, the old thing seems to be there still. You look all right. I answered: 'Yes, I feel great. It's amazing. I'm badly overweight, but I seem to be OK. I think I'll have a go again.' The other said: 'You must be mad. You're too old. There are a lot of good young fellows now.' That put me on my mettle and I said quietly: 'I'll have another go at it in time.'

However, when they went, I decided that there was no time like the present and applied to the Registry Office in Dublin for a jockey's licence. Stuart had been very good to me and I think this was more of a gesture to show him that I was willing to help in return, than any idea of making a second start in my profession. After all these horses we were training had to be ridden. I knew them and it might as well be me trundling them round the Irish racecourses rather than some chalk jockey who didn't.

Now, as in the early days at Lambourn before breaking my arm, the prospect of something definite to do helped me to control my drinking in a vague, limited way—not because I recognised that drink was responsible for my troubles, but because I knew that I was grossly overweight and that the calories in the alcohol I put back were largely responsible. Of course, I was still downing a steady quota of booze, because I had to have it and, for all my good resolutions, kept breaking out. In my loneliness I picked up a tramp off the road (we still have them in Ireland) and took him on a fierce drinking session. After that little episode I drove all the way home, blind drunk and blacked out. I will never know anything about that journey or how I managed to get right through the centre of Dublin, stopping at the traffic lights and so on. It's too terrifying to contemplate. And I can assure those who think that this form of amnesia is only the drunkard's excuse for his lapses, that they are mistaken. These blackouts were all too real and, in my case, all too frequent.

There was no doubt about granting me my licence on moral grounds. From that angle, I had never erred or fallen foul of the turf authorities and the name of Beasley, thank God, stood and stands as high as ever in Ireland and England. But, as I had not ridden for eighteen months, the stewards insisted on a medical check-up to ensure that my metabolism was all right.

With the weight problem in mind, I had already decided to consult Dr Austin Darragh, the Dublin endocrinologist, who had recently earned publicity from his successful treatment of Duncan Keith, the overweight English flat jockey. Unbeknown to me, Stuart had already discussed my case with Darragh, who had told him that no one could do anything about my refusal to get on a horse again. The decision must come from me, as it would in good time.

Now I went straight to Darragh, who chatted to me, did a few minor tests, and said he could find nothing wrong with me on the surface, but, to make sure, he sent me to the clinic at Cabinteely, just outside Dublin, for a more detailed investigation. Frankly I didn't give a damn, but I'd told Stuart I'd ride and I might as well go through with it for his sake. So I went. The clinic was staffed by excellent nursing nuns from a French order, who put me to bed and took blood tests, including cardiographs, and all sorts of other things. Having renounced the Pope and all his works, I felt a bit uptight about the nuns. They were good to me, however, and did what they could to ease my depression. My mind was willing—even wanting—to have a go, but I was feeling terribly low physically. I had no energy at all. As a result of his tests, Darragh discovered that all the Saluric, hydro-saluric and lassix tablets plus the alcohol had completely dehydrated me, turned my metabolism upside down and taken away all the electrolites, so that my nervous system was shot to pieces. He said there was nothing left. He also realised—and I took it from him, albeit reluctantly—that I was an alcoholic, but he didn't recommend Alcoholics Anonymous, because, although it was founded by a doctor and it undoubtedly works wonders, its methods are still (mistakenly in my opinion) mistrusted by some of the medical profession.

I told Darragh: 'I'm giving myself over to you. Whatever

you say, as far as I'm able, I'll do.' He suggested that first of all I must concentrate on reducing my weight and getting physically fit again.

A nun came to my bedside with an injection. 'It doesn't matter what it is,' she said. 'It'll make you feel better.' It was my first injection of perentolite to replace the lost electrolites and the effect was extraordinary. Suddenly the depression disappeared and I started to feel well again. So much so that I got up, went straight to a supermarket down the road and bought myself a complete set of new clothes. I wanted to live again. I felt that I was on my way back at last.

Darragh informed the turf authorities that I was all right and I received my licence. He worked in co-operation with an ex-boxer in the Montrose Hotel, called Eddy Downey, who had a health clinic and was later to become a great friend. Between them they had done miracles with Duncan Keith and they were using the same treatment on me. The immediate problem was to remove nearly $2\frac{1}{2}$ st in a short while and to make me fit.

I rode out and helped train the horses every morning at Portmarnock and, for four days a week I went in for saunas, exercise and, when Darragh considered them necessary, injections of perentolite and vitamin B12.

The first stone and a half came off fairly easily, but the remainder refused to budge. For three weeks nothing happened and I became very depressed, thinking that I would never break through that last barrier. But Eddy Downey kept encouraging me: 'If you can stick it, it'll come.' he repeated time and again. And sure enough by Christmas I weighed about 10 st 5 lb. I was fit to ride at Limerick. There was no idea in my mind about making a fresh start. I was away from home, working in an isolated sort of atmosphere with Stuart, and I thought that, if I ride this horse of ours, at least I'll have proved to myself and others that I've knocked off the booze, or at least, that I can control it.

But, of course, I hadn't and I couldn't. So I rode and the

horse went well enough. This was great. At least I'd done it, but I hadn't got to grips with the job. I was still just drifting along. The following week I rode him nearer home, at Thurles and we finished third. Next day there was a tiny piece by Tony Sweeney in the *Daily Mirror* headed: 'BOBBY IS STILL GREAT'. I read:

> Jockey Bobby Beasley, who recently came out of retirement, finished third on Gordon in the third race at Thurles yesterday.
> Beasley impressed the crowd with his riding and showed that he had lost none of his old skill.

That did me so much good. Perhaps something might just happen . . .

Soon after this I was at home for the weekend when Nicky Rackard rang up. Francis Shortt had broken his leg in a bad fall and Paddy Murphy, my old friend who had given me my first Grand National mount on little Sandy Jane, was looking for a jockey to ride his horses. Nicky had suggested me. I said: 'No, I couldn't. It's too much for me,' but he managed to persuade me.

Now, at long last, like a blinding light on the road to Damascus, I somehow knew that the moment had come. Darragh was helping me; Eddy Downey was helping me, Stuart Barratt was helping me and Paddy Murphy was going to give me a chance. This was my moment of truth. I suddenly knew for the first time that I didn't just drink too much—I was actually powerless to control it by myself and must seek help to knock it on the head and stop it once and for all.

I rang Nicky back. He said: 'Right. Come to an Alcoholics Anonymous meeting with me tonight.' I went and I thought the whole thing was a load of rubbish. There were about two dozen men and women from all walks of life. The chairman gave an address and read out the principles of Alcoholics Anonymous for the benefit of new members. He explained that there were no fees or dues, no religious ties, no political affiliations and that it was all open and free. The whole idea was to help people with drink problems just as he, himself, had had, and to give a feeling of fellowship and belonging. Anonymity was complete, No surnames—just Tony, Dick, Harry, Joan.

Then an experienced member gave an address on a certain theme pertaining to the beliefs and principles of the organisation perhaps examining one of the Twelve Steps in depth. After he had answered questions, the meeting seemed to be thrown open naturally and everyone who wished talked about his or her problems, described experiences and asked questions. As each one had finished speaking, others discussed the problem and some were able to offer advice, or, frequently, practical help. Finally, late at night, we all had a cup of tea and went home.

'Well?' asked Nicky. I said: 'Jesus, they're all mad. I felt I was the only sane person there. They *have* to be mad. How could twenty people all have the same sort of symptoms?'

I didn't want to go again, but Nicky persuaded me. After all, it was I who had stopped *him* drinking. And look where he was now—a sober, practising vet again. I'd asked for help and he'd shown me where to find it.

So I accompanied him to the next meeting and the next and the next. Same thing. No effect. Rubbish. My mind was closed. I wasn't even listening. I was still feeling self-righteous. I felt that they were different from me. They were much worse than me. I couldn't identify with them.

Then, as we drove back home from Wexford after the fifth meeting, I said to Nicky: 'OK, I understand. Now I'll admit that I'm an alcoholic too and will try to follow that programme.'

So, at the next meeting, when it was thrown open and the chairman looked in my direction, I stood up. 'My name is Bobby,' I told them. 'I am an alcoholic.' I had overcome the biggest barrier of all. I had admitted that I had the disease, which is at last recognised as one of the world's greatest killers. Nobody can get on to the road to recovery unless he has

admitted that he is not just an excessive drinker, but an alcoholic. Even today people keep trying to persuade me that I am
not one, but I know that I am.

After that admission, my mind was released and I told them,
as far as I could remember, all that I had done to wreck my
life. No one was in the least shocked, although I suppose
most of them knew who I was. They neither condemned nor
condoned. Here at last were people who understood because
they too had reached rock bottom. They too had come to
Alcoholics Anonymous as the last resort, desperate, even
suicidal, with nowhere else to turn. And through my story, as
through theirs, ran the same theme, and the same symptoms
—escapism, resentment, guilt, remorse.

They convinced me that alcoholism is not a weakness of
character, but an incurable disease. At least with cancer you
either die or are cured. But with this disease you can live for
years, wrecking other people's lives as well as your own. It's
like an atomic missile lying on the launching pad, a powerful
destructive force, which is quite harmless until it is activated.
The booze is the lethal warhead. So there is only one answer.
Don't put in that warhead. Keep off the booze for ever. And
from the moment I accepted and admitted the fact that I am
an alcoholic, that is exactly what I have done.

The biggest problem I had to master was the guilt and the
remorse for the frightful emotional damage I had done to my
wife and our marriage. I think this was the worst thing of
all, learning to live with the fact that I had been such a bastard.
It was not going to be easy to live a constructive, sober life with
the ever-present knowledge of the past.

The factors that most effected my reform were the desire
for it, the admission, the identification with all the other members, the programme, and one particular idea—'Just for today'.
This presupposes that it is impossible for an alcoholic to say:
'I'll never have another drink,' and keep his resolution. Never
is a long time, so is a year, a month or even a week. But one
day is different. Yesterday has gone, tomorrow doesn't exist.

You live for today and just for today you can manage not to have a drink.

The programme consists of following the famous Twelve Steps, and it is really important that one should do so while thoroughly understanding them all. But I have managed with the first two steps alone.

1. We admitted that we were powerless over alcohol—that our lives had become unmanageable.

2. We came to believe that a Power greater than ourselves could restore us to sanity.

For most people, like me, brought up in the Christian faith, (although I still reject Irish Roman Catholicism), this Power is God. However, AA rightly stresses that it can be any outside influence, which the sufferer regards as greater than himself. For me it is also my children.

I learnt that I must keep busy all the time. Idleness is as conducive to drink as pressure. Highs and lows, resentment and elation must be avoided. No hurry, no worry, just a steady even keel. However long one has been off it, it is necessary to keep going to AA meetings. It's a very easy programme once you get used to it, but it mustn't be used as a crutch.

I was to find that people, particularly in Ireland, became jealous of my teetotalism, and, in a way, let down, because they had enjoyed reviling me as a drunken bastard. They said: 'No, I won't buy you a tomato juice.' But as I've been abused and called every kind of sissy, it no longer worries me in the least. Then there are the vultures, waiting to see if you'll break, and wanting you to go back on the booze, so that they can say: 'I told you so!' It's just human nature, I'm afraid, to prefer villains to good people. In my naïveté, I never realised how many shallow folk there are in this world.

You quickly know who your real friends are. As soon as he learnt that I was making a comeback and riding Norwegian Flag for Paddy Murphy, Lord Fingall immediately engaged me to ride his top-class 'chaser No Other in the Leopardstown Chase on the very day thirteen years after I had partnered his

Roddy Owen to win the same big race. These are true friends. It was fitting that the comeback should start at Leopardstown. It received maximum publicity because many of the English Press had come over to weigh up Irish chances for the National and for Cheltenham's big meeting.

Two furlongs from home in the Stillorgan Hurdle, I thought that Norwegian Flag, on whom I was hard at work, had no chance until I looked at my rivals and realised they were going no better than my chap. This was too good to be true. I picked him up, doubting whether there was anything left. To my surprise I found that there was. I wasn't the same man that had ridden those feeble finishes for Fred two years ago. The old Beasley was back. I sat down and rode him out with all my strength. Three of us jumped the last hurdle upsides but I landed just in front and 'rode like a demon', in the words of one paper, to hold off two late challenges and to win to tumultuous applause.

This was the psychological boost that I had needed and I was able to reward Lord Fingall's faith by giving his horse a good ride to finish fourth, just behind L'Escargot in the big 'chase. He was delighted. Then, as for the rest of my career, there was no hanging about on the racecourse. I changed quickly, got into the car and drove straight home.

On the way I went through a little town, which contained one of my favourite pubs at a cross-roads. The lights were red as I approached and I thought to myself that I could just do with a gin and tonic. But, even as I slowed down, I was thinking when those lights change to green, I'll drive on and I won't miss what I haven't had. The lights obliged, as I had known they would. That was, oddly enough, one of the very few times that I have ever been tempted. I am acutely conscious of the fact that I will always be only one drink away from Hell.

I knew of a big businessman, whose company had a million-pound turnover, but who lost the lot through booze. Rehabilitated with the help of AA, he worked his way right back to where he had been and did not drink at all for twenty years. One night at a festive dinner, his business associates, well-primed with liquor themselves, were knocking him for not drinking and told the waiter: 'We'll have four more bottles of wine and a glass of orange-juice for the little boy!' He'd been taunted enough and forgot everything. 'I'm not a little boy,' he said. 'I'll show you bastards! Bring me a bottle of wine.' That evening he became pissed out of his mind and within a week he was in hospital.

I've come in for a lot of abuse. 'Look out, boys. Here comes the archangel, the Saviour, Holy Joe himself!' I haven't a halo. I'm no saint going around in shining armour, protecting people from booze. I'm just as big a bastard as ever. I'm a teetotaller and if anybody comes to me for help, I'll do my best. Nicky Rackard has saved five men from dying of drink. I reckon that's something to be proud of.

Immediately after Leopardstown, I became inundated with offers of rides and, although I had not started until two-thirds of the way through the season, I ended up right up among the leaders with twenty-one winners, including the famous John Jameson Cup at Punchestown on Dim Wit, which prompted Tony Power to write: 'Now it can be truly said that Bobby Beasley has completed a brilliant comeback to race riding.'

That Punchestown race sticks in my memory because I had to go into the bar afterwards. Believe me, I couldn't get away from all that rubbish quickly enough. It's only when you finally give up the booze and start to live, that you realise how much time people waste in bars.

I was now working hard getting the farm organised and, what with that, schooling horses, riding work and going to Darragh and the saunas, I found that I had a very full life. The next season was just as successful. I found that the Irish trainers were treating me as an equal and were always asking my advice about different animals, eager to get the benefit of my experience. Then, my old friend Pat Taaffe produced this remarkable young hurdler, Captain Christy with whom, in the 1972/3 season, we won four out of six races, including the Irish Sweeps Hurdle, which I described in the opening chapter, and the Scottish Champion Hurdle, smashing the course record at Ayr, as well as finishing third to Comedy of Errors in the Champion Hurdle at Cheltenham. Yes, I was back at the National Hunt meeting again just as Joe had predicted. I made a special point of returning to Sid's Bar in Leamington to have a good laugh with him about it and to thank him again for all his help in those dreadful distant days. If I hadn't held him up and gone too slowly, Christy would have won that Champion.

I'm often asked if I got the same thrill out of riding during my second start. The answer is that I got a decided thrill out of it, but that it was quite different. I wasn't the same person and I didn't look at it in the same way. After all my experience in England, where so much more is expected of you, it was in one way easier, using that experience to defeat the young and inexperienced, and in another, more difficult riding in Ireland. They all knew I had this drink problem: some knew I was an alcoholic, but, not understanding alcoholism, they were constantly watching me, waiting for me to slip back. After the Sweeps the lads, who used to sit with me in the saunas, were, I'm told, betting £50 at a time that success would put me back on the booze in six weeks.

How little they knew. Now I was doing a job—the job that I could do better than anyone else—to re-establish myself, restore my self-respect and make some money.

And, with the money that I earned from the Sweeps, I built a cow byre.

All the slaps on the back meant nothing. After reaching rock-bottom, I had no more illusions, no cockiness. Going through the mill of racing, I was only too conscious of its effect as a great leveller. One minute you're up and the next you're down. AA had taught me to keep going on an even keel as best you can.

I'd had visions of doing something with the farm and expanding, but they were only castles in the air. At least I had put off the idea of getting cows and starting milking until some later date when I would have more money and a bigger place. However, at an AA convention at Nenagh, I was still listening at half-past three in the morning. A man was saying that he was always procrastinating—even in a small way. He wanted to expand, but, as he knew he couldn't, it gave him an excuse to put off all his plans till tomorrow.

So the very next day I went out and bought seven heifers, determined to make a start now with what I'd got rather than wait for a nebulous future.

As I didn't know much about cows, I went with a friend, who was an expert. On the way back from buying the heifers, we stopped, as is the usual practice, at a pub—any excuse is good enough for a drink in Ireland. I gave him his large brandy and ordered a tomato juice for myself. When he came to buy the second round (that's a pernicious habit) he said scornfully: 'You're not much of a man, are you? You're a bit of a bloody sissy drinking that girl's drink!'

Like talking to a child, I explained quietly: 'The mere fact that I'm on tomato juice is the reason why I'm here buying heifers. If I were drinking brandy like you, I wouldn't have any money or be in any position to buy them or anything else.'

He left me alone after that. This is an attitude that you have to overcome. You have to become completely selfish about sobriety. It doesn't matter who tries to influence you, upset you or run you down. You must gain that inner strength from knowing that nothing on earth could ever be as ghastly, as horribly depressing and terrifying as going back on the booze again. Every rehabilitated alcoholic must be so selfish about sobriety, that it can be hurtful. If a friend, even a wife, interferes, he or she must go. I knew an alcoholic couple. The man had worked like hell, with the help of AA, to stay off the booze, but the wife missed her parties and the bright lights. So one night, when she was half-cut at a party, she spiked his bitter lemon. 'You're not a man,' she laughed, 'just a bloody wet.'

He ended up in hospital and the marriage ended in divorce. So you must be utterly ruthless and selfish.

Captain Christy is the most brilliant jumper in training. But, like many brilliant people, he is not quite as others are. Even I, who knew him better than anyone else, admit he is a little bit crazy!

In his first novice 'chase at Clonmel, he gave me a hair-raising ride. It was one of the most exciting races of my life, if you like that sort of thing! He took charge and, jumping like a wild thing, hurdling his fences at great speed, left the others miles behind. At one stage, he was three or four fences in front and, although he almost took the last out of the ground, he won as he liked.

He was a bit better, but still scatty, when we went to Punchestown in November and won the Wills Premier Chase Qualifier.

Later the same month, we took on my old friend Bula in the Black and White Chase at Ascot, where I'd ridden my last big English winner. Christy had travelled badly—like his jockey, he sometimes seems to lack electrolytes—and sweated up beforehand, so that he was in a terrible state and was not going as well as Bula when we came into the second last. So I thought that I must jump that one well, to have any chance, and, forgetting that he was a novice, I was sitting too far up his neck, and I asked him too far off. He put down and I went on without him. I'd paid the penalty for over-confidence.

When he got home he coughed and he wasn't a hundred per cent when he took on Comedy of Errors again in the Sweeps Hurdle on Boxing Day. He ran a great race in the circumstances. I tried to make the running, but he was never firing that day. He just wasn't the same horse. Half a mile from home he was out on his feet and it was only dogged determination and guts that carried him into third place.

So we went back to England for the final of the Wills Premier Chase over those drop fences at Haydock. The ground was too firm for him and I let him go on. I wished afterwards that I'd held him up, but he was standing off and really pinging his fences. Coming to the second last, he was a certainty, but he was tiring and I said to him: 'It was my fault at Ascot. This time I won't ask you for a long one.' He put in a short one, hit the top of the fence and, deceived by the drop, came down.

Coming back to Manchester airport with Pat in the taxi that evening, I realised how much store I had set on the Cheltenham Gold Cup and I was terribly depressed. It was my fault that we hadn't won at Ascot and Haydock. I'd let my horse down as well as my old friend Pat. This was the first real test of AA's teaching because, normally, after that sort of day I'd have drowned my sorrows. It never even entered my head. As I got into the taxi beside him, I said to Pat: 'Jesus, that was a desperate day!' He, too, was sunk in gloom. I shook myself mentally. No depression. There's no point in going on the booze for something that's gone. That's a negative attitude. You want a positive approach. Go forward. Attack. I asked: 'When's he in again?' 'Punchestown, in a fortnight's time,' said Pat. 'Great: we must get him back in the groove again. You'll run him, won't you?' Pat agreed and sure enough he won. We gave him one more race at Thurles, and he cantered in, although he almost smashed the last fence to smithereens, and we were all set to pit our novice against the best 'chasers in the world at Cheltenham. And I am sure that I was the only person in the world who knew that, if things went right, Christy could beat them all, including Fred Winter's Pendil, and Fulke Walwyn's reigning champion, The Dikler.

Christy's trouble at that stage of his career was that he was still trying to hurdle the big fences—and he was a horse who really used to bend his hurdles—but, when he hit one, he was so quick he could find a leg to save himself somehow. Unfortunately, his head would disappear completely and, as he hadn't much of a neck, you'd find yourself with nothing at all in front of you, which was apt to be disconcerting to say the least. A remarkable horse.

I paid my routine visit to Darragh, who knows about racing and, as part of his treatment of me, had studied Christy as well. He told me: 'You must go into very strict training and get yourself really tuned up, because this horse is so quick that you must have the reflexes of a young man.' That is what I tried to do.

In order to save expense, the owners sent Pat Taaffe and me over to Cheltenham on a package trip. So, as the two of us were having breakfast in a strange hotel away from the usual racing crowd at the Queen's, we were able to have a lengthy open discussion of our tactics in the Gold Cup. I suggested: "Let's surprise them all by holding him up. They'll be expecting us to go on and they think we have very little chance in any case. He'll jump better settled. We know that he gets the trip and that he has plenty of speed.' Pat agreed that we should let him settle down, play it cool and have no set plan.

I doubt if anyone who was there will ever forget the National Hunt Festival of 1974. The weather was like mid-June and, looking at the huge, happy crowd and the sun-drenched hills in the background, I thought that there is no more glorious place. Christy had travelled well and, despite the heat, he was as cool as any of the runners as we paraded in front of the stands. Somehow I managed to blot out of my mind all memories of Ascot and Haydock as well as the opinions of the 'experts', who gave us no chance. I knew that, if I could organise him, Christy would win. This was the one day that Taaffe, Darragh, Downey and Beasley had been working for. It was a fresh start. I turned to canter down completely relaxed and free from all pressures at last. It was up to me.

Charlie Potheen jumped off in front with the rest of us bunched up behind at a moderate gallop. Coming down the hill for the first time, I was about a length behind the American horse, Inkslinger, when he fell and so nearly brought me down. His hindlegs caught Christy's forelegs and he stumbled badly, but he recovered and was jumping beautifully, nicely settled down.

As we turned for home at the top of the hill for the second and final time, I planned to sit behind The Dikler and Pendil until the last fence, knowing that we had the speed to beat them on the run-in. I had been tracking a horse called High Ken, but, for some reason, I didn't like the look of him. My experience told me that, when the tap was turned on down the hill, he might be a bit dodgy. So I moved to his outside.

Sure enough he fell at the second last and brought down the favourite, Pendil, who was tracking him. I heard the crash and realised to my dismay that, with Pendil gone, I now had only The Dikler to lead me to the last and he wasn't going quite fast enough. I cruised upsides with Ron Barry and Christy met the fence perfectly. I asked him and . . . he put down, hitting the fence hard with his chest. Once again his head disappeared, but this time I was ready for him. I picked him up, balanced him and passed The Dikler on the run-in to win quite comfortably. But for that mistake, he'd have won on the bridle.

They sang 'When Irish Eyes are Smiling'. The cheers as I rode in were deafening and very flattering because they came from thousands who had lost their money and were applauding me personally. It was marvellous and I was very grateful.

CHAPTER 15

Life is for Living

Probably I was now more hardened and cynical. Even in those moments of triumph at Cheltenham, as the crowd gave three cheers for me, I was thinking less of the actual victory than of my gratitude to AA and the others who had helped me to knock the booze and to use racing as a means of rehabilitation.

And, when they held a celebration party in Dublin's Shelbourne Hotel, there were still some folk who expected me to break out. As it was, I reckon I showed as good form as anyone —on bitter lemon. It just didn't enter my head to sacrifice a lifetime to one night that would soon be forgotten.

My new-found cynicism was justified when Christy, the favourite for the Irish National at Fairyhouse, fell at the sixth fence. Pat ran him again the next day and, as I went out on him for the Power's Gold Cup, all the adulation of Cheltenham was forgotten. I was roared at and booed by people who seemed convinced that I had deliberately engineered that fall and I asked myself what's it all about? This is a load of rubbish. I've done what I set out to do. Living is more important than racing. I'm nearly forty and it's time to get out.

So I set Christy alight, jumped off in front and made all

the running to win. As it turned out, it was my last ride on him.

At first in the euphoria of Cheltenham, I had been offered a retaining fee of £1,000 to ride Christy in the following season. I had accepted because this would go a long way towards paying a cowman for my expanding dairy herd. Even when the offer was reduced to £500, I reluctantly agreed to carry on for the sake of Pat and the horse. But when the owners said that they couldn't afford this, I decided that the time had come to call it a day and to look after the cows myself.

The well-deserved publicity for Stan Mellor's record total of 1,000 winners had already convinced me that my 800 represented a fair career in all the circumstances.

I went to an enormous AA Convention at Thurles. There were nearly 1,000 people and, if anyone wanted proof of the terrible problem posed by alcoholism to the world as a whole, and to Ireland in particular, it was there. There was a bishop, priests, nuns, doctors, lawyers, members of every profession and every walk of life from leading businessmen and rich women down to road sweepers and tramps. Both sexes, all ages, including, sadly, a large number of teenagers. There was no discrimination. They all had the same problem. Without the help of AA they couldn't master booze.

It was a great night. There was dancing and even a bar, so that if anyone had wanted to get drunk, he could have done so.

There are two types of alcoholic, chemical and emotional. The former, of whom Willy O'Grady was a perfect example, drink for drink's sake and keep going until the body gives up the unequal struggle. They are the plodders. The emotional ones, like me, are the sprinters. Willy O'Grady never harmed anyone. But the emotional alcoholic, who probably doesn't actually like drink, but takes it as a drug, has his or her exaggerated highs and lows and can do immense harm to families, friends and self.

The R.C. Church in Ireland and the country as a whole are slowly waking up to the terrible problem they have created. Through their distorted religious unbringing, young Irish boys and girls are too immature to withstand temptation. On the one hand drink is glorified. The TV ads have us believing that young men can't get girls without a special lager or some other drink and 'social drinking' is still often an excuse for a booze-up. You're not considered a man if you don't drink and you are supposed to be a real hard man if you get paralytic for hours and take days to recover.

On the other hand I'd like to see more Christianity and less of the strict religious attitudes towards alcoholics. It's not a weakness of character, it shouldn't be a stigma and it can't be cured with the old recipe 'give him no money and plenty of work'. It's a terrible disease, which takes control of you. Ordinary events are seen as crises and drink is seen as the only salvation. Society must be educated to trust the rehabilitated alcoholic, who is normally an almost annoyingly conscientious perfectionist, and neither to condemn him in any way, nor offer him temptation. I have lectured the admirable new apprentices' school on the Curragh on alcoholism and on the many pitfalls which lie in wait for young jockeys.

From a personal point of view, I find it very difficult to live with the hurt that I have done, particularly to Shirley, and here we are up against one of the major problems of rehabilitation. In common with other emotional alcoholics, I will always urgently need affection and yet, in my bad drinking days, I battered, possibly irreparably, the sensibilities of the wife who was prepared to give it to me.

Alcoholics Anonymous has a sister organisation called Al-Anon, which tries to study the woman's side and to help the wives of alcoholics to understand their husbands' problems. Perhaps one of the most difficult things for the spouse of any reformed alcoholic to grasp, is the sudden switch of sympathy. For years your sufferings have been somewhat allayed by the comforting sympathy of your friends, confirming your own justifiable belief that you are nothing short of a saint to put up with such a horrible drunken bastard/bitch.

Then suddenly you find the roles subtly changed. The former bastard/bitch is now admired by all and sundry for knocking the booze and you are married to a hero/heroine. This is far from easy to take because you, too, feel you must forget all the past and join in the admiration and encouragement.

Then, rehabilitated alcoholics are apt to be moody and selfish and you realise that the former monster, who has ruined your life, is now in genuine need of a love and affection, which has long since evaporated. Yet, if you don't provide it, you will be condemned as an unforgiving so-and-so.

Shirley has read a lot of Al-Anon and we have frequent discussions about the problem, but she is still having great difficulty in understanding. This is not her fault. It is a fact that no psychiatrist is any use to an alcoholic except a psychiatrist who is an alcoholic himself.

Shirley and I find it very hard to communicate on the problem. Of course it is possible that we were not really compatible in the first place. She's an introvert and I don't know how badly she has been hurt psychologically. I wouldn't blame her if even Time, the great healer, proves incapable of healing this particular rift. While I just don't know how she kept her sanity, I do know that stability of background is as essential to me as close-knit affection.

After the Gold Cup, I had shoals of letters from alcoholics, saying: 'We read about it and the knowledge that it could be done has given us a lot of hope.'

And Austin Darragh, to whom I owe so much, says: 'You've no idea how many silent thousands you have helped by admitting your alcoholism publicly. You could so easily have blamed your bad days on falls, overweight, etc.'

I only wish that I could have helped my wife as much in return for all that she has done for me.

Our son, Peter Beasley, shapes really well on a horse. But

I am ensuring that, when he grows up, he will be more of a businessman than his father, and that he will be emotionally mature, fully equipped to cope with all the various hazards of a jockey's life. I want him to be dedicated to life—not to racing, which can so easily get on top of you if you let it.

I am eternally grateful to Fred Winter for his compassion and understanding. He said to me the other day: 'I couldn't fathom the fluctuations in your riding. One day you were excellent and the next day horrible!' I deeply regret letting him down and also failing those other trainers who did not understand the problems of alcoholism and will probably always think of me as 'That temperamental sod, Beasley'.

My grandfather at one time owned 3,300 acres at Skerries House, Athy. Today I own 30. I am now milking twenty-five cows and had my work cut out during the golden summer of 1975, which brought the worst drought in living memory to Wexford.

One day, all on my own, I was trying to fit the milking machine on to a heifer for the first time. God, I thought, she kicks worse than a thoroughbred filly! And my mind flashed back to the English jockeys' changing-room as I wondered which of my old friends would have been a help. I could have done with big, blond Terry, the Gloucestershire farmer's son, as she kicked and spurted dung all over me from head to foot.

When I had eventually fixed her, I stood back exhausted and a vision of a smart, smooth, saturnine suburban jockey suddenly caused me to burst out laughing, as I said aloud: 'I wonder how old Mouldy would cope with this situation!'

Postscripts

JOHN OAKSEY IN THE *SUNDAY TELEGRAPH*—
DECEMBER 31, 1972

Sad as it was to see Bula beaten last week, the Irish Sweeps
Hurdle had in other respects a supremely happy ending. For
by winning it on Captain Christy, Bobby Beasley gave his own
irrefutable answer to the old defeatist moan 'They never come
back'.

Three years ago, struggling unhappily and unsuccessfully to
make a living as an insurance salesman, Bobby, who had
known the heights of success in the jumping world, had the
sour smell of the scrap heap in his nostrils.

Battered by falls, failure and increasing weight he had lost
job after job, his marriage was, for the time being, on the
rocks, and the rides had dwindled, then dried up altogether.
So finally in desperation he turned away from the world which
for almost 20 years his skill had so brilliantly adorned.

It didn't work of course: it very seldom does, because for
men who have ridden the violent switchback of a jumping
jockey's life, a 9–5 job away from horses is pretty much like

aspirin to a mainline addict. For Bobby Beasley, I suspect, it must have been even worse than most.

His own temperament had always been a switchback—soaring to heights of hilarious Irish charm but all too easily plunged back to pessimistic melancholy.

I have seen him set a whole party ablaze with gay self mocking wit and mimicry and I have also seen him sitting on the weighing-room bench staring grey faced into nowhere, with defeat hanging round him like a fog.

To most of his friends the defeat seemed absolute and final when, in despair, Bobby went home to Ireland. Competition for rides is even fiercer there and anyway his weight was still sky-high.

For the solution of that problem Bobby has to thank Dr Austin Darragh, the remarkable Dublin specialist who in the past few years has pared and dieted innumerable jockeys down to a racing weight and in most cases kept them there. But Dr Darragh's treatment, however successful, is never more than half the battle and, for Bobby Beasley, it was even less than that.

It remained to convince both himself and a sceptical world that he still had something worth while to offer as a jockey. In that long fight Bobby had several weapons on his side —notably the goodwill of friends with good memories like Captain Christy's trainer, Pat Taaffe—and of course his own inflexible determination.

But the most important of them all was the detail that he has always been and happens to be a truly great jumping jockey, one of the half-dozen best all-rounders in my opinion to ride in the last 30 years.

To go with strength, a cool head and utter fearlessness he has, what's more, an elegant classical style—something with which if they will forgive me, the contemporary Irish scene is not especially well provided.

Beside some established (and doubtless highly effective)

jockeys in their 20s, Bobby Beasley, at 37, looks like Nastase playing in a weekend country house tournament. On Captain Christy last week his tactics were as flawless as his style. And, as the Irish cheered them home at Leopardstown, a perfect seal was set on one of the bravest sporting comebacks since Ben Hogan.

The Twelve Steps

1. We admitted we were powerless over alcohol—that our lives had become unmanageable.
2. Came to believe that a Power greater than ourselves could restore us to sanity.
3. Made a decision to turn our will and our lives over to the care of God as we understood Him.
4. Made a searching and fearless moral inventory of ourselves.
5. Admitted to God to ourselves and to another human being the exact nature of our wrongs.
6. Were entirely ready to have God remove all these defects of character.
7. Humbly asked Him to remove our short-comings.
8. Made a list of all persons we had harmed and became willing to make amends to them all.
9. Made direct amends to such people wherever possible, except when to do so would injure them or others.
10. Continued to take personal inventory and when we were wrong, promptly admitted it.
11. Sought through prayer and meditation to improve our conscious contact with God as we understood Him, praying only for knowledge of His will for us and the power to carry that out.
12. Having had a spiritual awakening as the result of these steps we tried to carry this message to other alcoholics and practise these principles in all our affairs.